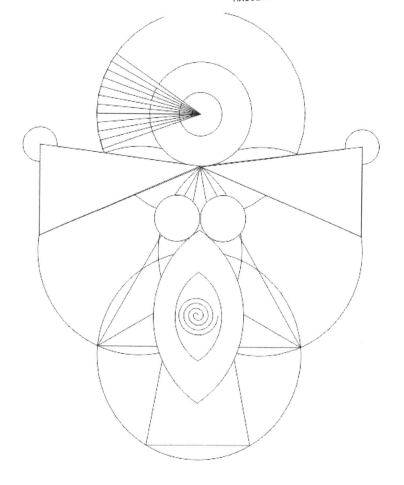

The Goddess Unveiled
© 2019 Richard K Page.

SOLOPHI.COM

The Goddess Unveiled

This book is dedicated to the ladies that shaped my life

Earth
My mother Joyce, whom I owe my large heart.

Water
My wife Elizabeth whom I owe by backbone and strength.

Air
My daughter, Iona whom I owe my joy.

Fire
My sister, Julie who I owe my tenacity.

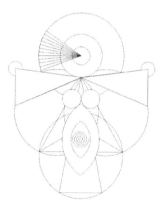

Goddesses all

The Goddess Unveiled

Contents

The Goddess Concept

Welcome to my mind for the period of this book. Excuse me if I proceed immediately without introduction and without as much build up as I have previously done. I think enough basic tuition on this old process of thought has been done in my other books, and if this is your first, don't worry, it's all very simple. In fact, half the issue we have with understanding ancient concepts is that we layer them within a framework of modernity. As you would if you were beginning a meditation, clear your mind of preconceived knowledge and existence, allow the words to flow into your mind in a very basic and uncorrupted manner. Upon reaching the concluding paragraphs of this book allow yourself to then bring in the critical thinking and judge the work as a whole.

Pagans, witches and others interested in the Goddess, please don't be discouraged by my frequent references to Christian and Hebrew god concepts, the book uses them as a platform to establish a syncretic relationship, remember you've claimed that Christianity is stolen pagan values, well to establish that we have to present a lot of Bible passages and beliefs, and then place them back correctly into their pagan context. There's a lot of it "in the beginning." that is also there for our Christian readers to be able to build on their framework too. Beliefs of others are not your enemy, this is doctrine more closely aligned to religions. To truly take yourself away from the dogma of religion, you first have to dissolve the framework of religion which preaches that all other theosophy that strays from their doctrine is the enemy.

No, hidden within that text as you claim is the source material of ancient, more syncretic truth.

I think this is the time to assume my readers are not beginners in the subject of the esoteric method of thought process that I have catered to in the past. Our minds are modern and vexed with the complexities of that modern life; ultimately this leads us to place modern templates onto the understanding of our ancestral origins, which is a large part of our failing to give them credit for their genius.

The human of old did not think like we; they had more clarity of thought simply because those complexities we carry with us every day are ingrained into our very core thought process. Their world was smaller, more immediate and the cause and the effect of the life experience they encountered, from their immediate surroundings, culture, ideas, philosophies, and those stretching out into the cosmos had less of a spectrum of expressions between them. And so, the correlation to an expansive universe and their innermost conclusions were much less divided by intricacies than we perceive today.

Often, we underestimate the knowledge of our ancestors too readily. What we call art in its most scientific form from back then was far superior in terms of elegance to the mathematical structure and science than that which we have today I would suggest. Consider this artistry in workmanship in the same way as our buildings. If we looked at a country manor house being built five-hundred years ago and a country manor house being built today, what you will see is this transition of science from the aesthetic and more permanent solutions, to the disposable, functional and less creative solutions applied to the requirements of the building. In the same vein as I said above, the mind worked differently and its purpose was moulded differently, perhaps too much for us to understand them fully and that arrogance may very well be why we quickly assume superiority to our ancestors in terms of progress, yet where we have progressed in some technology, we have most assuredly lost out in elegance and understanding of hidden principle and ideas which underpin the creativity of our distant relations of ages gone by. For every one of us here today, we have relations who lived in the periods we cannot truly understand. Roman times, medieval times, all the way back to shamanistic and superstitious little gatherings around a fire, barely knowing how to use tools, we all came from that! We all have a bloodline of strange and exotic cultures which are the source of us, and therefore the source of our substance today.

The modern house will be technically, mathematically and scientifically a much more functional home than an iron age roundhouse, without a doubt. But it will not last anywhere near the time of many of the buildings of antiquity, nor will it be seen with the same reverence in say even five hundred years. Your ancestors, even the near historical ones, thought differently, not lesser in terms of complexity, they had little collective access or availability of knowledge, books and the wonderments of other people's discoveries we now see as simple facts of life. This information was never as readily available to research as they are now, yet they still had the same brainpower that we have today, just directed in a way that was more conducive to their needs and environmental issues than we do. We have isolated ourselves from mother nature; we rarely care for such things as a bad harvest, winter stocks, or how a minor injury or ailment could lead to death.

For us to quickly grasp the prehistoric concepts, ideologies and the later evolved values that have brought the modern characters of the goddess back into mainstream culture as it grows with women being more liberated than in near history to dispose of the father god which has been imposed on us all. Men and women are beginning to open up to goddess concepts, thanks to the equality movements, the goddess it seems has been an unintentional benefactor of modern values, which in reality is ancient values, hidden by a dark age of the church and its persecution of anyone who does not toe the line.

Unfortunately, the long time that the global domination of a male god figure has held prominance, has almost rescinded the goddess figure to folklore and fairytale. And when we try to find the source to this ideology, we find it has been hidden from us, and it is presented as simple mythology or comptemptual quaintness. The Goddess, with a capital G, still does not get the grace and respect of any of the mainstream religions male counterparts.

This is not by accident; your lack of sources and reverence has been purposely eradicated into the stuff of mythology. But let me assure you, that by any names the Goddesses may have, and any planets and stars they are portrayed to represent, they still do not get the accolade attributed to the monad in his male role, let me further assure you that this was not always the case. Our ancestors, closer to nature in every way, could see something in nature and in the cosmos which required both male and female equality on a universal scale. What I hope to do with this book, is to begin the insights into the Goddess that I believe is at least a foundation of ancient concepts long since lost.

First, we begin by affiliating the 'Mother' character as a universal representation of all things that are 'Material' and so 'The' goddess with a capital 'T', is all things in the universe which are physical, structured, measurable and observable.

The Universe and we, are binary systems. 1 and O, those numbers aren't coincidently representative of our physical genitalia, it goes much deeper into existential natures and symbolism than that. Also important are the letters I and O as representing the same thing. We tend to think of the 'one' as being something, and the 'zero' as nothing, but that is just an example of modernity and its thinking. While the concept of a number zero isn't documented as being a mathematical construct until "invented" by the Hindu astronomer Brahmagupta in 628ce, the absence without mathematical equation was considered less of an absence of subject, than an equal opposition to all things that have presence. When you balance the absence of subject to the presence of a subject you can see that absence is much more present and significant a form of the universe than things that are present.

A series of 1's and 0's collaborating provides infinity. One of the solid principles of ancient knowledge or gnosis is a very simple idea that when "one", "I", "self" or "spirit" enters the three-dimensional physical universe, we are in a vessel which we call our bodies. That vessel is the material (maternal) aspect of this polarised universe, and therefore feminine.

The spirit is masculine. Although I am male myself, my body under this law is 100% female, this is not a sexual declaration, it has nothing to do with fundamental sexuality, in reality, its more just a hermetic method of division and aligning one concept, "sex" to number, to the letter, to existing and not existing, to black and white, anything that has an absolute polar division, simply gets aligned male or female, they're all just representative of a concept.

This is as simple as it gets at the base level of understanding most of what the ancient books are trying to tell us. Of course, we get more complex as we introduce divisions in each of those base principles. And those infinite possible divisions within division go on to make the unique us as individuals, where no two are the same.

So, let's ignore the orthodox default rhetoric taught to us for so long which are aligned to the Goddess by the Historians, and Theologians as you will have read a million times before. I desire in my books to bring my readers new thoughts rather than reinforce their old ones with symposiums of dullness from the orthodoxy they can find on Wikipedia any day of the week.

The rhetoric from these historians which places seemingly all goddesses as being representative of beauty and love, and fluffy bunnies…I think a Goddess deserves more respect than to pander to the patriarchal dominance which seeks to undermine the feminine constructs which are the true Gods of this Physical Earth as we stand today. If one could try to summarise the feminine energies instead of merely describing them as physical in a scientifically observable phenomena, then gravity is as close to her expression as can be.

We are on the cusp of the restoration of the Goddess as a supreme deity, as is her place in the universal cycle of human consciousness. Paganism is in resurgence, and this is ordained to be, immutable, unquenching thirst for balance cannot be stopped like the sea.

Know that, all the universe is a system of flows, waves and cycles, and we ride a wave of ebbs and flows between two tremendous and wonderous opposing forces which themselves are just more examples of this binary universe made up of something and nothing, but most importantly all the glorious expressions which lie between. Such beauty and potential within we can barely imagine.

These expressions between, are what we could simply call positive and negative influences towards, or away from further generated extremes of themselves, as I said, we could call them male and female, black and white, blue and red, past and future, yin and yang, big and small, inside and outside or even good and evil. This is where the binary concept creates an infinite array of sub-binary expressions. All things express themselves in a spectrum as they converge into infinite complexity between these things, and 'You', 'conscious thought', are simply the embodiment of the experience of the current convergence between them all at this moment in time.

You are witness to the universe; without you, it is dead!

While good must oppose evil, that does not mean that evil is necessarily the negative consequence; it's a subjective consequence. Without that evil balancing good, we would never know good, and without this binary opposition, the entropic decay of the universe expressed in these violent oppositions of opposing factors would be the true death, a grey where nothing can express its uniqueness. Good needs bad, is not new thinking, so moving swiftly onwards.

It is true that the greater expression of any evil, must by a universal harmony create the greater expression of an equal good.

The Mother or Goddess at the highest archetypal order is aligned as I suggested, with the material rather than the spiritual universe simply based on these terms. All opposing elements have an alignment, the list above we could say the female is yin, the female is black, female is evil, black is evil, black is yin, it doesn't matter as long as an alignment is reached.

Culture shapes our default alignment of these; the church has made female the temptress of Eden, its common to fear the dark, so evil becomes black, as in "black magick". Black-Magick is considered the de facto "evil magick". But in our context, these cultural alignments don't matter. Suffice to say; you just need to understand the alignment of one to the other.

If your familiar with the bible, then you have Cain and Abel, one good, one bad. Does it really matter what their names are? One was a shepherd, the other grew wheat, between the two their opposition is further defined by their jealousy of each other, their constant vying to be the favourite of their father, a metaphor for a god figure. The two were given dominions over metaphoric meat and vegetable; the dichotomies just need to be present, and so when you are reading ancient texts or trying to find esoteric meanings in things, try to think in this binary state of mind. Isolate the people and their activities from their base constructions. This alignment isn't static. This is where the cycle comes back into the picture. As a wheel turns, one half is on top, it rotates, and that half goes to the bottom.

Empires will be built, and they will fall. the Sun rises and the Sun must set, life begins and ends. What happens between is our spectrum of observation. In the patriarchal past aeons, man has ridden his wave of superiority as it was due, now it's the time for the rise of the feminine aspect to take its place in the cycle. But, that won't be overnight, the wheel turns slowly. Our ancestors knew of these cycles, which incidentally brings in a third element, the passage of time, Chronos. The Crown! Which assigns dominion over the current portion of the cycle which sits at the top of the conscious mores. But we don't need to worry about that too much for now. It is now in this age of Aquarius, that the cycle brings in the feminine wave of superiority and success for the goddess revival, which will at some point wane as man's has, and the cycle will begin again. What this will bring about is a step towards a more material divinity, gods will become more material and evidential. Now, you may have been indoctrinated into believing that materialism is a negative trait. But that's just another way our minds like to align these dichotomies into abstract metaphors, and probably influenced heavily by your patriarchally affected experience to date; as the patriarchy has been acquiring providence in a spiritual mechanism for over two-thousand years. Materialism is a greater custodian of The Earth, for example, rather than trying to profit from The Earth and its limited resources which the spiritual mind is incapable of conceiving as a finite source. The maternal, feminine instincts of materialism will nurture it into growth and the bountiful reaping of the harvest, she is the harmonised balance of spring and autumn, opposing the divisions of mankind's winter and summer months.

Wealth! Money! Cash! Well, that's not materialism, no,no,no! Money is patriarchal as it is ethereal, used to obtain material wealth. Money is a fabrication or concept without physicality. If you have $1million in your pocket right now, you may feel wealthy, yet in its truest form, it is only the idea that you are wealthy that supports the value of that currency. Currency's fail, and they will, very soon, I assure you, the goddess will see to that, money is flawed, and the material goddess will allow people to see through its artificial and illusionary state of being.

The Mother (Material) opposes Spirit (ethereal) which represents her male counterpart or mythologically represented cohort, but like all good marriages, they need to be made of opposing elements to broaden the horizon of the experience. In this capacity, the Goddess lends herself to all quantifiable science and measurable concepts more readily than she does to ideals of a more insubstantial and patriarchally natured manifestation of spirit. That is not to say that there is an absence of spirituality in the Goddess, but a more manifest-able and determinable state of observation of 'the mother' at work than there was in 'the Father' whose work takes him away from home, the father who once returned, his wrath is to be feared for it shall come with punishment for misdeeds in the day. Using traditional clichés, the product of a male and a female is a child. To the child, tradition shows the mother being more practical and present in the child's subjective experience of reality. The father, distant and absent. Could this be any more an analogy of our understanding of God's presence? This concept of the family structure which is now more and more rejected in modern society isn't coincidental; it is engrained into the very fabric of universal construction, which is why it seems more natural. But it is also humanities nature to reject our nature because temporal consciousness exists only in the tiny friction between the god and the goddess. To reiterate, under the older gnostic principles, if it can be measured, if it is substantial and quantifiable, then it is conducive to the feminine goddess principle of nature. The goddess is productive, creative and physical; She is cyclic, dependable, regulatory and reoccurring. She is present!

The physical aspects of nature such as earth and water are both feminine archetypes which form the first of the demi-goddesses under the 'The Prima Materia Goddess'. When we split out first binary state in the primordial alchemical elements, water and earth are the feminine components, fire and air, masculine. And of these divisions feminine Earth opposes Masculine air, as Masculine fire opposes feminine water.

She, like the Abrahamic "G" who is represented in the above diagram as Alpha, does not seem to have retained a name in the modern-day which comprehensively captures her higher authority as the uppermost archetype of the goddess. We commonly call "God" Yahweh, but we also know that "god" has other secret names, and those that have been hidden are the feminine aspects as "God" holistically is not male or female, but both, and that is the concept behind "gods" self-creation that will not fit comfortably into the masculine patriarchal version presented by current mainstream religions.

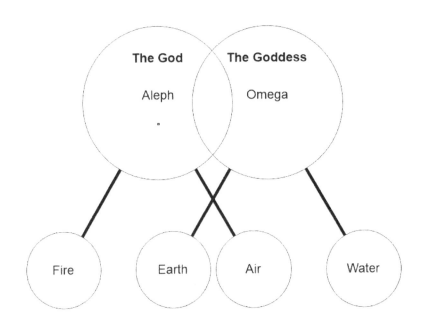

Or maybe, if I'm a little less jaded and sceptical in my opinion, and I try to be more objective, then maybe it has just been lost in modernity. Quite possibly it is now a name which we have associated with modern deities, spirits or saints in such a way that she has lost only her Prima-Materia status as a supreme mother goddess and her status in the collection of feminine aspects we know as a collective view, as mythological puppeteers of the human theatre.

However, her presence, although hidden remains in some biblical texts, such as when God speaks. Seemingly some of this feminine aspect to God slipped past the scrutinous eyes of the church's translations, or maybe it was intentional and hidden in the writings which we call "hermetic texts".

Hermetic, meaning sealed or secret wisdom. In revelations 22:13, God says "I am the Alpha and the Omega, the first and the last, the beginning and the end." This probably harks back to the period of the Christian-Gnostics, which don't reflect the Christians of today. The omega is a direct reference to the feminine archetype.

Fragments of her, survive with many names which relate to specific aspects of the expression of this overreaching archetype. These colloquialisms in name-use act as filters which constitute the parts that in reality, make up the whole. These names then seemingly separate the Prima Materia into different goddess facades such as   Lilith, Eve, Maria, St Anne, Dianna or Nut and many others are all aspects of this single source mother goddess monad, but with different personalities or areas of ordinance dependent on the specific nurturing needs of the society and culture that created them. In this book, I will try to relate her back to many historic incarnations as they are all-encompassing. She constitutes all base elements which have infinite potential for creation and creativity.

To begin, below you will find the alchemical symbols for both water and earth respectively, which I'm sure you, my expected audience, will have an extended interest in occultism to some degree which is beyond the requirements for the average person, and these symbols are most familiar.

 When we look at the many goddess characters, across most world pantheons, you will surely find that they have always been associated in some way with these material concepts. The primal concepts are often obscured by the narrative of a story, or the context in which they interact with the spiritual and paternal counterparts. But always and without fail, the stories present the feminine aspect as a representation of material elements. They will represent some order of temptation, possession, desire and loss, as these are the parameters of material experience.

This experience will usually follow a "Paradise Gained" and a "Paradise Lost" formula, where the feminine aspect comes into our experience due to love and desire, which ultimately like The Moon and sun, will denote our rise and subsequent fall from grace. Reflecting the spiritual vantage point of heavenly pursuits being deferred by temptation or pride, which brings us to our eventual fall. Even life itself follows this cyclic process, from birth to our apex of beauty, virility and vitality, to decrepitation, and ultimately death, due to "insert vice here", Your doctors will tell you whatever pursuit you enjoy will contribute to your premature death. The mechanism is as old as time, "do this" or "do not do that" or you will surely die!

Genesis!

Of course, the upward portion of this cycle, from birth to the apex is the masculine growth, and the feminine is the decline, sorry ladies, don't shoot the messenger, this is how its aligned and I'm not making these claims as a matter of instruction in anything other than how to understand lost gnostic esotericism. Which was written at the last decline of the feminine and so the texts reflect that. What we will now experience is the decline of the masculine archetype, but we don't have the supporting history for that as it last occurred over four-thousand years ago.

And so, in our current timeline we can witness the patriarchal descent, like the downwards pointing triangles pictured above, descent, and downward pointing is aligned with the negative energy flows. But know only too well, the equality and the importance of those negative flows, and as I suggested earlier, we are at the turn of the cycle. Ladies, your time is here, it's all about to become much more empowering for you all, it was destined to be, and all this will flip on its head.

The complexities of the universe are constantly dividing, this is why we call it divinity; the source monad is infinitely divided into all its component universe.

We start with the whole, the universe, all time, all existence, all there is. We then begin with the very simple oppositions beautifully displayed by the Yin and Yang symbol. But before we get to that let us display it in its first division, male and female, day, and night, good and

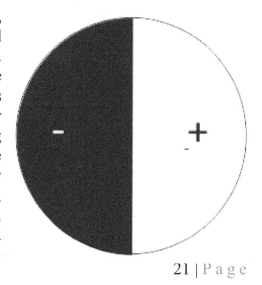

evil…whatever is your preferred primary division.

Here we have what initially appears to be a balance of oppositions. However, it is the highest order of division, and as you can see the white side if we imagine time itself, like a clock moving clockwise will only present the white side in descending, and the black ascending. This is imbalanced.

What we need is a more seasonal balance, where each gets its fair share of ascension and descension.

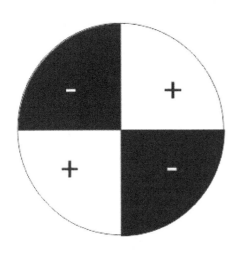

Now what we have, is closer to a universal harmonic balance, both positive and negative cycle periods will receive an equal balance of time in ascendance and descendance.

We can see the wheel of the year utilising such basic methods, a cyclic division of four.

- Spring – F- being potential and virtue in our above example. Cold but rising summer heat.
- Summer- M -Temptation, heat, lust. Apex heat,
- Autumn – F- an account, possession, wisdom, age. Warm but descending cold.
- Winter – M -Death, loss, coldness. Apex coldness.

The universal experience of all things, of course, is much more complex, so we divide our existence, like the year into ever-decreasing segments, like months, weeks, days, hours, minutes, seconds and so on, such is the universe divided from base principles. Time has provided us with more and more divisions which I referred to earlier as "complexities of modernity".

The male and female form the first division of all that is, the scientific singularity before distinction within itself. The male and female, represent that first cell division in the singularity and established light and dark which is based purely on a simple affiliation that is built upon a dualism or the dichotomy which presents all things being made up of elements and these elements are only identifiable by their presence within an equal yet opposite counterpart. Many Bible critics will question how God created light, then the Sun , when they think of creation as being The Earth in seven days, but that's not the "light", light was the first division in the singularity, thus yang had its yin.

All things have some form of polarisation in their expression. When you imagine this infinite division, you ultimately come up with something that looks like this (above), but each division merges into its opposing other as the wheel rotates thanks to that third element Chronos, the crown that I said we would get back to, which drives us along and turns the wheel of time.

The perpetual motion is better represented by the well-known Yin and Yang symbol, which is the same, a wheel turning, and endless cycle of the night into day, each defining the other by their presence, without one there would be no other.

This principle or universal law states that a single unity or 'singularity', must divide into opposing states.

And so strongly featured in Gnostic concepts we find that male and female represent the perfect metaphor for these opposing states. Male and female when viewed as originators of a concept, become mothers and fathers of those concepts, and each concept is assigned a metaphorical gender. This does not translate that the subjects in question are more prevalent in females or males, more that the aspects share attributes that are represented as female and male.

Now, you may think that I'm waffling a bit too much about male aspects in a book dedicated to revealing the goddess, but to reveal the goddess, you must as the yin yang symbol shows, you must know where she is, and her definition is also the definition of her counterpart, for she is where he is not.

I once tried to argue with an atheist that he must have a concept of a god, to not believe in a god. He didn't get it, but I'm sure other atheists will. But in short, to say there's no such thing as any god, one must define the nature by which you identify what a god is, and we all have a personal idea of what a god is, then we can choose where it exists or not. This is the same; the goddess is defined by the male counterpart, as she defines him.

So back to my opening premise, all things that are substantial (material) are female, all things that are insubstantial (immaterial) are male in this principle. And to create life, the male enters female. Now that isn't just a crude way of describing the act of sex. It reflects the wisdom of this gnostic concept. When the male spirit enters the female material, we have a life, you. You are in gnostic terms both male and female. Both positive and negative, you are a construct of two people of the opposite sex, merging and creating a new division.

No judgement is made of any hierarchy other than all hierarchies are equally comprised of male and female aspects and all subordinates also have equal divisions of positive and negative forces within them.

Whether you are sexually designated male or female, your parts are spirit, soul, consciousness, which are aligned with male properties; and body, blood, earth and liquid which are aligned with female properties. This can be seen about The Earth itself, land and water, The Earth is female (Gaia), other none physical components of what we call The Earth, such as air and fire, for example, would be designated male attributes. Using that rule, we can see easily why the Sun is male, the Moon is female. While we know now that the Sun is much bigger than the Moon, as luck would have it, due to the Suns distance from the Earth they only appear that they are exactly the same size, we then extend out, again our nearest planets, our neighbours living either side of our house.

Because consciousness is considered the ethereal and male gender, it clearly does not suggest that people designated as a female in their sex do not have consciousness, any more than Mars does not have "earth" elements that are the greatest part of its makeup, although I suspect if the ancients would've known about gas giants such as Jupiter, they would've been more selective on aligning those to the male structure, and the more solid planets female.

In understanding the pre-historic views of god archetypes. We are representations of our parents, which equally are comprised of a male and a female, your actual acquired intellect and your body could have come from either parent, as they too have both. The concepts are purely representational.

To assign gender to an aspect, concept or object, we look at the prime attributes of the object and place it into the construction of the gender which best suits its classification. You may wonder why Water and Earth are appropriated into the feminine division of the alchemical elements? Well, it is based upon a principle now associated with dark magick and what is commonly called the left-hand-path (LHP) but isn't exclusive to that idealism, you will surely have heard this axiom before, the phrase "As above, so below". This principle, of which I am a great believer, suggests that we humans, and all things on a microcosmic level, are a fractal manifestation of a larger macrocosmic extension of itself, within itself, within itself and so on. So, based on this, we can find out as much about the nature of the grand universe by looking at the infinitesimally small components of it as we can by attempting to see something far beyond our reach.

Supporting this, the atom and its operation bears a resemblance to the solar system, the solar system bears a resemblance to the galaxy, the galaxy is merely an atom in the universe, and who knows how far that continues outward beyond our current capability to see. So, we look within to find the answers to that which lies without. This principle seemed to work well for our ancestors, and I honestly cannot find fault with it today.

The Earth, when studied by our ancestors, bore a striking similarity to the nature of a woman. She was attuned to the worldly synchronicity far greater than her male counterpart. Her cycle reflects the cycle of the physical moon. She bore fruit, the offspring of man which in very simplistic observation is comparable to the fruit of the Earth, who will later be called "Mother Earth". She became in a very rural dependent timeframe the fertile field unashamedly "ploughed", a phrase in old English terminology for procreation and embedding the seed into The Earth which went on to produce new life in the most miraculous universal form of summoning the powers and elements of nature and the beginning of a universal Magick. There is no doubt that under ancient concepts of divinity, that despite the arguments of patriarchal religions of today that the mother was the creator god archetype, but a mother cannot conceive alone, so in gnostic creationism, the father would be the provider of the seed or the architect who without the material mother was. Our singularity like cells dividing, identify the opposing forces within itself which creates a division, from which all other divisions must be fractal subdivisions of. The male father must, however, be gestated or formed within the mother, so even if we do resolve the question of our immediate god…then we only open up a new chapter of asking who created God? The Gnostics, freemasonry even the very male orientated catholic church all identify "the mother of God".

The two symbols from the four base alchemical elements shown earlier are of the feminine downward pointing triangle. A symbol is closely resembling the fertile post-pubescent female pubic area, a 'V' shape. The letter "V" itself is pronounced as you know "VE", phonetically "vey" which is Yiddish for "woe" and misery, as in "oy vey" which means "oh woe" and how we English speakers ended up with the word Wo-man, the aspect of humankind who bears the burden and labours of childbirth which is the human manifestation of life itself. Life, of all the wonders of the universe, is beyond question the most miraculous, mysterious and magickal concept we can imagine. Ve crosses continents in its meaning, yet roots to similar concepts of Life, Light and Love. I find "ve" to have an essence of a very motherly aspect of possessiveness in the "bearing" capacity too, to "convey" is to carry a message, to "have" is abbreviated as a possessive "they've" for "they have". For example, even the word possessive has that ve on the end, and in such is not the essence of the word "possess" in its capacity to remain the owner, but "possessive" is almost "passi-ve" in its context almost being a temporary bearer of the article, which really fits well with the archetype of a mother concept who bears her children for a while before they become independent of her in their growing stages of life. The Ve-nus, hints at being born (another root of bear) is the "sun" in reverse into "nus". The mother of the Sun , bearer of the light, Venus.

The breaking of waters reflects the basic understanding of the universal concept, where there is water, life can exist. But the origins of the association to woman and water is engrained in symbolism, language and letters from every spiritual ideology around the world. The 'W' (double Ve) which forms the beginnings of life and the words woman, world and water are based on the formation of the wave. The symbol we see is that of the waveform which is all expressively feminine. This is particularly pertinent as we stand at the dawn of the age of Aquarius the water-bearer, who is surely a woman and the logical progression from the patriarchal aeon brought in with the fish of Pisces that we are just now leaving behind, the new age is upon us. The age of enlightenment, like the goddess Venus brings in "Ve" in her capacity as "to see" in its old-French roots "veoir" where we derive the word "video" or the Spanish "Vista" meaning to view. It can be seen, therefore the objective "View" of something is feminine and alive "viva". In fact it becomes "very" difficult to expose synonyms with the feminine "ve" concept without using many words which intrinsically contain the letters "ve", "vi" in terms of illumination of truth. We must "believe"! The word "wave" itself, reflects greatly as symbolic language root, "Wa-Ve" links with "wove" which in the act of weaving is the process of creating a waveform which goes, o-ve-r and under another wea-ve. Indeed, the title of this book, "un-vei-ling" hints at the re-ve-lation of the concept that the root of "ve" is a depth of understanding which becomes illuminated only when one searches through a "veil".

In Hebrew V and U are one in the same, which is why we call it a double u and not a double Ve as our Germanic based English language would dictate, English is heavily rooted in Latin, Germanic and Hebrew, although the Hebrew isn't spoken about as much as it should, its almost as though, it been eradicated from our history books. And one has to question if this is to hide the Goddess embedded into the language. If you look up the etymology of any English word, they all seem to root to middle English, Germanic, Latin or French maybe occasionally Greek, and yes, we can see that, however throughout my books, you will see that I find most of these hidden gems of esoteric meaning, by breaking down the syllables and aligning it with Hebrew phonetics.

In Hebrew U and V's meaning is structured like a link which exists between two objects "Vauv", objects which are divided by the dichotomy. Object-Subject-Object.

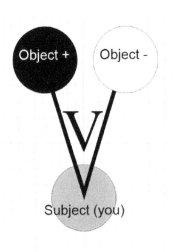

The shape itself is a symbol of this concept. What V creates is a subjective link between three definite articles. Once these letters were ideograms, which over time have been superseded as phonograms. But it is by trying to understand the origins in the ideograms and the phoneticisms that we can gain greater insight into the minds of our ancestors and their concepts of gods.

It is important to understand that the simplistic view that we hold today of the *what-exactly-the-goddesses-are* is wholly incorrect. Primarily the modern "goddess" was created by the rhetoric of orthodoxical scholars and facilitated by opponents to heathen and pagan belief systems which included feminine divinity.

Often their lack of understanding was founded in one-to-one relationship with objects and their representations. They simplistically attribute our goddesses to concepts such as fertility, war, famine and love, trying hard to box the Goddess, into a fixed and rigid framework, rather than the "all things" which they like to present the father god as.

What that has resulted in, is confusion which makes the idea that events and consequences that we attribute to acts of gods, sound ridiculous, fanciful and metaphoric mythological tales. Yet despite their efforts, within ourselves, we seek a truth contained in these representations if only to express ourselves as part of that deific genus. We align ourselves to a patron goddess, with the intent of imbuing her characteristics within ourselves. Surely if that essence of the character is appealing, then we honour that god, not as an object, but as an essence of the archetype. The orthodox method looks at either the Object+ or Object- in the above diagram and tries to present a fixed association to one or the other and the god after which it is named. In truth, a god, or goddess as per our chosen exploration, encompasses not the objects individually, but the dualistic relationship between the two. This is why the planet Venus, and the Goddess Venus are polarised in their meanings. Goddess of Love (Morning Star), Goddess of War, the Evening Star.

Venus herself is unchanged as an object, but as a subject, she can be interpreted quite differently. In fact I would suggest that the war attribute of Venus, is actually male, but because modern scholars see the name Venus feminine and war, they assume Venus is feminine, but she isn't, she may be considered feminine when she gives birth to the day in the morning, or as she drags the Sun down

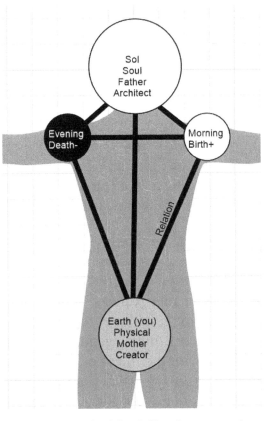

into the underworld by temptation in his fall of an evening. But she could also be considered male, penetrating the skies in the morning and dying in the evening in a celestial or heavenly war falling as Lucifer, to which we start the next day cycle in "mourning" for. Were all for want of a better word hermaphroditic (the hidden Aphrodite) as holistic lifeforms.

We microcosms of the solar extension, reflect that status in our personality. Consider yourself, are you good or evil? Are you strong or weak? The subjective answer to all those questions always lies from the view of the observer and their concepts of good and evil, or strong and weak. And to this extent, the cyclic nature of life and the rotation of the Sun is another expression of the [1]anthroprocosm.

Looking further into the formation of letters and their use to present a meaning which is universal, one could suspect that the ancients had a good understanding that light itself could be presented in waveform, this is important to my explanation, you will see as we continue that I feel the zodiacal symbol Aquarius to be more correctly presented as "the wave-bearer" rather than its oft expressed "water-bearer" for reasons that will evolve as you progress through this book. To get you to loosen the rigid definitions that have been placed on gods and goddesses so far, I would like to explain the way our mind works by default, as opposed to how it needs to work to better grasp esotericism in general.

It is a consequence of modern interpretation and the modern minds framework that there is a need to quickly relate objects on a one-to-one relationship to a spiritual deity, architype, demon, planet or star. This is principally where we often go wrong, as we should be considering each as a sphere of influence or the forces which exist between two expressions of objects. I'm not claiming that in all cases a one-to-one relationship is wrong, but it is not correct either. For example, remember I said that all things are divisible, then so is "tuition". Tuition is past tense, it comprises of firmly established concepts which can be locked down to be disseminated as valid and often repeatable knowledge, it is

---

[1] The relationship between the self and the cosmos. As above so below.

masculine because it "enters" you from an external source. The feminine counterpart is "in-tuition", knowledge which conceives the future, coming from the inside and expressed outwardly creating the drive which leads us towards development and creativity. Intuition is the essential ingredient of wisdom, intuition works in the same area of consciousness that wisdom resides, however wisdom is the application of that intuition, reinforced with "knowledge" as experience.

Creativity is the feminine genus from which gnosis is equally obtained and what creates. The goddess is not one of those simplistic one-to-one relationships between object and meaning, but some complex inner workings of cycles and positions which when presented in certain orders, creates greater meaning. If that sounds complicated, let me assure you it's not, you have been using its feminine methods throughout this book in a very short few pages to this point.

I have spent some time explaining to you the hidden depths of the phonetical sound "vey" or "v", the same principle can be applied to planetary and astrological alignments as they can in words "leaver" and "reveal" all use the same physical components, by which I mean their letters "aeelrv" presented in alphabetical order, they are nonsense. Yet in certain positions, and places they can reveal very specific and very different meanings. What we experience with the current presentations of the goddess is that nonsense. We only see the letters in a one-to-one relationship where each letter has a specific meaning and the orthodox will present that meaning according to their intent, placing the order to reveal the words as they want you to see them. You should consider each letter both unique as an object in a word, but each word a collective subject of letters. Also, realise that every letter and number have a shape which reveals yet another meaning. You will then begin to see a lot more of the manifestation of the Goddess revealed in her name. The image a couple of pages back extends the simple concept of the observation of the dualistic nature of Venus to include the other great object in our skies, our star "Sol". We are a combination of Soul and Body, Spiritual and physical, consciousness and matter. The imagery somewhat resembles the manifestation of an upper torso.

So far, we have linked symbols W and V with the aspects of feminine symbolism, remember even letters, as familiar to us as they are today, were all once complex symbols with unique aspects as pictograms like the Egyptian hieroglyphs, letters today have lost their pictographic origins and we rely purely on their relationships with their surrounding letters in words to generate meanings phonetically. But every letter has three layers of interpretation, pictographic, phonetic and the word value. Stop! Look at the letters in front of you, those shapes aren't simply there to distinguish them from other letters. Every single one of them has its own pictographic meaning like the snake "s". When was the last time you saw a letter as an independent glyph?

Then phonetics which is usually grouped in syllables which are constructed in sets of three, this is a rule but not a law. The next logical letter that presents itself in wave form is the letter 'M' which begins many words that are distinctly feminine, mother, madame, matriarch, matron mama and maiden. M (mem) too, is a symbol representing the waters, from which all things come, if you look into ancient creation stories, the land often emerges from the waters, as children break the waters in their birth, the word "birth" (berth) itself, is still heavily associated with water vessels.

The system of waves in modern physics is half of the duality of reality as we perceive it. Light itself is made up of either waves or particles. Even now while we look at quantum physics as being the next frontier of the understanding of reality, we find embedded into our study, that the words which seemed innocuously named "waves and particles" have these masculine and feminine attributes. Particles being male and masculine sounding phonetically similar to Patriarch meaning father, or testicles and waves which I have already elaborated on. I'm sure you're familiar with the story of Moses who "parted the waves". Maybe if I do a book on patriarchs and gods, I'll go more into detail of that. Suffice to say that anything beginning "PA" is most likely masculine, from papa, pathology, paternity. Actually, paternity is a good one, remember I said that male was an architect, "pattern", "patent", do you see how that fits whereas female was a creator. If you have been seeking illumination for a while, I hope this puts you on the right path of seeing things that have always been there, hidden and by very definition "occult" as the goddess unveils herself.

The next letter which is heavily associated with feminine aspects is the letter 'S' which when looked at in its form rather than the meaning which has been forced into you, it is simply another waveform but standing upright. 'S' is associated with water, from both its waveform and the concept of the river, winding its way across the land, bringing fertility and life as it passed through. In Hebrew, the letter 'S' is known as 'Shin' or 'Sin', and it is written a very similar way to our English 'W', in fact in Proto-Hebraic, it was even more resemblant of the English and Phoenician letter 'W'. Apologies if you're not familiar with my work, be prepared for me to dance all over the place with language, symbols and pantheons, as I am an ardent believer in a syncretism between all spiritual beliefs. That is what I write about, it is with the intention of breaking down the walls creating division in people merely for the sake of the name of their theistic patronage. Trust me, whatever gods or goddesses you believe in, they exist in all the other belief systems too, under different names. And I jump about so that no matter from where your spiritual experience lies, you can see the associations in other pantheons.

Meanwhile, 'S', back on topic, you can conceive of this shin symbol appearing like three rivers, pouring into a sea. The 'S' symbol as a waveform, viewed sideways returns to a crest and trough configuration we call a sine-wave (sin). I hope you're picking up on all these phonetic similarities, The sinewave is one of the fundamental principles in science as an observation of the ebbs and flows of reality, and using the "as above, so below" principle it is essential in observation of celestial bodies which feature heavily in ancient mysticism; which are most often named after the gods and goddesses of antiquity, or is it more accurate to say the gods and goddesses are named after the planets? Or, are they one in the same?

Before we move on from the Hebrew structures of these letters there is also the lower case 'S' which is written in Hebraic as

And from that, there is the cursive version which resembles the English lower case 'e'

In cosmic creation symbology, this is also expressed as the spiral. You can see the spiral galaxy reflected in this simple design strongly associating a cosmic creation which is gnostically thought to be feminine in its construction. This  brings us to an important word for you to contemplate to begin our journey into the earliest mother goddesses, 'galaxy'.

The word 'Galaxy' comes to us from the Greek 'galaxias (γαλαξίας)' which translates to "milky" and is the namesake of our very own galaxy, "The Milky Way", not the coolest name we could've conceived for our little corner of our universal home I admit, yet did our ancestors know that our galaxy was just one of the billions of galaxies in the universe as they viewed through only their natural eyesight the spiralling shapes of other distant galaxies? From our earthbound view the milky way appears only as a long arch of a more densely populated star stream which collects across our galaxial axis. Well I think it's pretty evident that they did, because the word I used there 'galaxial' did not require the word 'axis' afterwards, axial is contained in it and in the original Greek 'galaxias' the axis is implied. History and etymology seemingly will not support the clear evidence contained in words as we see them every day, familiarity has bred contempt, and dissecting these words is the key to understanding esotericism and revealing the veil of the occult. The occult in question is to unravel the knowledge of our ancestors, which to date is becoming more and more apparent that they knew a lot more scientific principles than we give them credit for. Evidence suggests that civilisation and the science associated with it has been "forgotten" or purposely erased. Every day we discover tools, equipment, concepts and structures which make us ask "How did they know that? Given our understanding of their civilisations, the timeline simply does not fit.

The Milky Way is indeed a strange name, I hope you have ever had opportunity to be out on a clear night with low light pollution to experience the majesty which is the horizontal plane of our own galaxy, spanning the middle of the night sky, how glorious and wonderous it is, if the night sky be a goddess, then for certain no other has more absolute beauty. If you have not been so blessed then I'm sure if you search the internet for images of our galaxy you will see many pictures, none will really do it justice, but I'm sure you will understand what we see, is a representation of that spiral shape lay down flat on its side, like looking at a plate, not from the top but bringing it flat up to eye level, on which we rest on an outer section of the spiral. So, from an earth view, it looks simply like a band of stars. How could ancients know it was one of the spiral galaxies?

As mothers, the feminine creator nurtures her offspring and her milk is of course, the natural provision of that sustenance. In humans, we politely call the vessels of this sustenance the breasts, in other animals and in vulgarism we have the "Teat" and "Tit". The letter 'T' being prominent in both words. Now, indulge me to convert that letter into a symbol. And look downward towards the nipple and areola or imagine a cow's teat. You see a similarity to the letter 'T'. I will come back to it later but also imagine a symbol if you can which is that shape front on.

There is, of course, a Hebrew letter called "Tet" or Phoenician "Teth" which of course represents the letter 'T' which looks like this. You can see in the Paleo-Hebraic and Phonecian something similar to our lower case t or a cross with a circle or halo around it, somewhat like a wheel or a Vikings shield.

| Block serif | Block sans-serif | Cursive | Rashi | Phoenician | Paleo-Hebrew | Aramaic |

In Phoenician its pronounced 'Teth', which means wheel. Supporting the principles of the cyclic nature of womanly virtues, and the wheel, which manifests itself in our galaxial rotation.

The word 'wheel', shares its roots with the words "Well" (in two forms), "Whole", "Holy" and "Halo".

'Well', in its two forms well can be used is phrases like "Are you well", "are you well-nourished", "are you nourished from the well" and continues into common phrases like "the well of life" and "the wheel of life". Wells, of course, being somewhat comparable to teats from the nourishing mother earth and her underground rivers.

The Goddess Within.

The goddess is the physical representation of the universe. She is personified beauty, for men as well as women.

You have developed a daily routine, which is the cycle of the feminine of all earthly presence, like the Sun rising in a morning so does the goddess, slightly before her masculine counterpart.

As children at birth, chi continually ebbs from the cycle of life, our energy peaks like a child in the morning of its life.

Add to your daily cycle of routine morning exercise above all other forms of exercise. Thirty minutes fast-paced walk or jog at the moment of waking, before anything else even before the breaking of the fasting (breakfast) is the most beneficial, beyond all other exercise and stresses in the day.

The physical attributes of the beauty is hidden by the toxins of the rest of the day's toil.

With each step, consider your place to be the circle in the symbol below, and each step forward is the move towards a positive result in the cross, as time passes the greater the pace, the greater the effect.

With each right step breathe in the future, and with each left breathe out the past. This will regulate the pace to your need for ox-y-gen. All the time imagine yourself when you felt your best when you were at the peak of your physical attractiveness.

Adhere to this routine for 362 days, and you will regain the beauty of the Goddess as your mind will reform the image of yourself that you know lies within. From day one, happiness levels will increase.

Of course, there is nothing new here in terms of exercise is good for you, but what is important is the conditioning in which you perceive the ideal self.

Maybe you have lost faith in yourself, but the goddess is incorruptible of doubt.

Have discipline!

The Bovine Goddesses

I went to pains to use the word Ox-y-gen in the above lesson, but the segue into this chapter was irresistible.

As humankind stared at his celestial companions, the crescent moon followed the body of the galaxial centre belt across the expanse of his evening skies. Upon occasion it fulfilled itself to its round, whole and complete form, and in its labour birthing the new moon whose crescent formed the horns crowning the head of the celestial bovine queen.

Bo, usually a Latin suffix, means to grow or appear. **Vine,** as in vineyard, is the branch of the tree, from which the fruit grows.
Bovine - an animal of the cattle group, which also includes buffaloes and bison. Synonyms: cow, heifer, bull, bullock, calf and ox.

Let's look at the word broken down. In Aramaic it is called "Bet" our letter "B" and is the second letter of this and many other alphabet constructs including our very own English in line with its gematria value of two.

In the Hebraic language, it makes either a B or a V sound. Bet and Vet, as bet it means 'House', symbolically it is a "bovine head"

If we now look across to Egyptian mythology we will find that there was a goddess whose name was Hathor. Hathor was the source creation goddess from which all other gods were derived. Dating back to the astrological [2]Age of Taurus, Hathor is depicted with the head of a cow. I will quickly throw in some more phonetics I want you to absorb that I will come back to later, Taurus (T-Aura, T- Horus, Thor and of course Horse).

The Taurean age (4000 to 2000 BC aprx.) was an age of great enlightenment for humanity, it was when first evidence of human industriousness began. And what better symbol for the industrious age, when mankind began to make his environment work for him, instead of relying on the provisions of the gods? Mankind began to cultivate the environment to provision his own destiny, farming relied heavily on cattle which could work the fields, domesticated beasts such as cows, oxen, horses and goats became the desirable currency of prosperity. Hathor was not represented as an agricultural god, however the reliance on these types of animals can certainly be considered a step away from the reliance of an external entity. Mankind in his most simplistic terms was replacing the benevolent god provider with his own mechanisms of success, more reliable and measurable than devotions and sacrifice.

Hathor has later been linked to the more commonly known Egyptian Goddess Isis, Nut and the much less well known

---

[2] The Age of Taurus – The Age of Growth. The Age of Taurus spans approximately the period between 4400 and 2200 BC. It is the age defined by the Sun being in the constellation of Taurus on the spring equinox.

Mehet-Weret, all of whom were also depicted with cow symbolism.

I don't know about you, but I find it inconceivable that a pantheon would have multiple gods sharing the same concepts, yet this is what historians will present since they are restricted to their actual but limited evidence. Unlike myself who is free to present a more conclusive framework based upon a holistic narrative. History cannot make assumptions, and that is how it should be, yet like science, theories must be conceived, and then allow the evidence to support or reject that idea. The truth is for you to decide rather than be instructed. I'm a firm believer in personal truth being decided by the individual rather than having it thrust upon them by declaration "this is a fact", if we stuck with that, we'd all still be burning witches. Unlike the material nature of the feminine aspect, concepts such as spirit, love and consciousness are unquantifiable and to me must fall into a more masculine aspect as I described earlier. Yet, love and other inconsequential and unquantifiable experiences are thrown as a tagline on goddesses like it's a defacto state, "it's a goddess, so it must be a goddess of love or fertility", to me that's lazy, and doesn't fit as many goddess energies that they try so desperately to ingratiate into that entity.

Mehet-Weret, is probably the least known Goddess mentioned there, yet is critical in my presentation. Mehet-Weret was called the Goddess of water and creation, conducive to our theme, in addition to other representations, she is ascribed the title of the mother of the Egyptian god Ra. Now Ra (masculine) is labelled as a Sun god. In my personal understanding, I would say not quite, but a "light" god, and the origin of our word "ray" as in "sun ray". This forms an important distinction as sun rays are ethereal, and without mass, and therefore [3]masculine.

Mehet-Weret was the cow goddess who gave birth to light, similar to another well-known pantheon whose first creation was light, and he saw that it was good. Now, on our solar-system based observations, the mother of light is the planet Venus, again we will get to that later.

So, while we have a mother of our localised Solar centre in Venus, there is a higher order to the Galaxial centre in which Nun is the whole of the skies. Even in the day light, the skies were Nun, mother of all which exists within her. To this day, mid-day, we call the mid-day sun "Noon" establish a relational concordance between time and space, something we consider to be state of the art "spacetime" Theory introduced by Albert Einstein in 1905. Here in Egyptian Mythology we have the principles of the dimensions extending into a fourth inseparable state of conditions which define a whole.

What we have now is almost like a stack of Russian dolls, a mother, within a mother. As above, so below. So, these representations within the single pantheon of Egyptian mythology are not the same Goddesses, but a hierarchy of principles which present a universal creation story beyond that of the limited earth centric view.

---

[3] **Mas-cul-ine**, to cull or kill mass, the end of mass, 'Mass' a measure of matter, being feminine, -ine suffix meaning pertaining to, so 'pertaining to not-matter').

According to legend, Mehet-Weret was responsible for raising the Sun into the sky every day, Mehet Weret was a bovine creature who's significance lies in her deeds and her form, this is all that really matters when we wish to get a better understanding of the iconography applied to Gods and Goddeses, not who they are, but their deeds and those deeds help to define their iconic depiction.

The Sun, is preceded in its sun rise by the morning star Venus, which in many pantheons is known as the light-bearer, carries the light or pulls it like a chariot across the sky, and in philosophical and esoteric concepts is a metaphor for the bringer of light being "wisdom", "illumination" and "revelation".

Revelation being a very cyclic word, Re (ray, rah (male)) Ve (woe (female)) lation, which is now a depreciated word which until Copernicus decided that the Sun was the centre of our solar system and was "relatively" a fixed object, it meant the "motion of a celestial object from one place to another". Revelation literally means when the Sun moves and sheds light on things, and by association includes the toil of the bearer who does that duty. Often this beast of burden is depicted as either a bird, or a horse, or a bovine which pulls in its harness the Sun across the sky. Re-ve is light of the mother, I think the best picture I can place in your mind for this is observing the daylight moving across the earth as the earth spins, the lightly appears be in motion across the land, yet it is really the land (mother) illuminated by the light (father). The revelation is that moment in the light which we call a day.

Because it precedes the Sun at dawn, the Sun's light radiates from below the horizon and the break of actual dawn is preceded by a haze of sunlight in which the veiled planet Venus sits. To the Greeks this haze is known as PhospHorus (phosp-Horus, and Horus which was probably adopted from the Egyptian at that point, is phonetically similar to horse, yet horse is Germanic according to etymology). But etymology can only go as far back as written evidence suggests, the phonetics and sharing of spoken language predates by far any written evidence we can find. Also 'phos' meaning 'light' and 'pHorus' unsurprising meaning 'bringing' are incredibly similar by themselves, almost as though light and bringer can be merged, "bright".

Returning to the metaphor I mentioned a moment ago, the word philosophy is also Greek, the first half 'philo' which means 'lover' and sophos which means 'wisdom' both are male aspects incidentally. Even the word 'metaphor' uses meta, which is a physical construct, presenting a 'phos' insubstantial masculine concept. A metaphor constructs philosophical concept into a material comparison.

Sophia is the Greek goddess of wisdom, and wisdom itself with the feminine W starting it is actually a double V, 'Visdom' implies the domain of the visible. Light is shed upon that domain. The Hellenistic aspect of [4]Sophism. But

---

[4] A sophist (Greek: σοφιστής, sophistes) was a specific kind of teacher in ancient Greece, in the fifth and fourth centuries BC. Many sophists specialized in using the tools of philosophy and rhetoric, though other sophists taught subjects such as music, athletics, and mathematics. In general, they claimed to teach arete ("excellence" or "virtue", applied to various subject areas), predominantly to young statesmen and nobility.

how can Sophia or Venus be female under my premise if wisdom is immaterial? This again boils down to the physical object of Venus, bearing like a mother bears her child, the light. The light is the wisdom itself, Venus and Sophia, are the wise ([5]Vis, Visible) aspects of that wisdom.

There is no doubt that Horus (male) was a god of wisdom and light, like Ra. But we must assume that Horus being masculine cannot represent the physical nature of the planet Venus which is feminine, but the phospHorus illumination of the Sun or the light of the Sun itself, pre-dawn. Venus we are told is a goddess of love, love is not metric, its unquantifiable in nature so must also be masculine. It also penetrates the physical, which is a masculine trait. Venus, despite historical claims is not a goddess of love, but is absolutely conducive to the expression of love inspired in us. Venus the goddess gets its name from the Roman pagan pantheon. Ve-Nus, and like all goddesses it seems for historians is a 'goddess of love, beauty, desire, sex, fertility, prosperity and victory', but I dispute the prime aspect of love for the reasons above, Love is a masculine aspect.

Let's look at the word 'love' itself. Two syllables Lo-Ve, it is no coincidence that Ve ends the word love and begins the word Venus. Lo-ve-nus. And it is no coincidence that the second syllable of Venus is the word Sun backwards. 'Lo' roots itself with the phonetic "Low", please bear in mind that Venus is only ever visible low on the horizon due to its closer

[5] Vis-à-vis comes from Latin by way of French, where it means literally "face-to-face". In English it was first used to mean a little horse-drawn carriage in which two people sat opposite each other.

proximity to the Sun , when the Sun eventually follows it up, Venus like all other stars and planets are obfuscated by the light of the Sun . 'Lo' also suffixes the word "Halo" which is Ha and Lo. Hathor is also two syllables "Ha-Thor".

Thor we all know is a male God from the Nordic pantheon, son of Odin, brother to Loki. Odin, the prime father God of that pantheon is a one-eyed wanderer, incidentally the word "Planet" is Greek, for "wanderer". And to round off the northern European mythologies, I will quickly throw in a phonetic link to English mythology, Arthur (Hathor) who was the king of the twelve knights of the round (wheel shaped) table. So, before we stray too far away from our Goddesses into European masculine Gods, let's get back to Halo and Hathor ([6]heifer), what are they then?

Well the Latin word 'halo' which we commonly associate with hovering around the heads of angels, saints, Jesus and those people thought to be 'holy' and 'wholesome' is derived from the Greek word 'halos' which commonly means a disk of light which emanates from a celestial body such as the Sun or The Moon, the outer rim of a shield and 'hal' itself is off on a tangent but is actually the Greek word for 'salt' specifically of the sea, so feminine in the fact it is a mineral which comes from water. But also shares roots with "Hail" and "Hel" which are phonetically pronounced versions of the Hebrew letter E.

---

[6] **Heifer**, a cow that has not borne a calf, "A Virgin Cow"

However, the relationship between salt and its holy state becomes more apparent as its representation as Horus, the Horizon. And if we look at the English lower case 'e' we have almost an exact representation of the alchemical symbol for salt as seen in the picture right. Salt is the fifth element in the alchemical table as one of the acids and 'e' is the fifth letter in the alphabet, salt known as "Marine acid". Phonetically Salt shares its name with Sol, the Sun , Salute (to hail). Solve (Sol-ve) , becomes a great equaliser, the solution which is an inevitable cycle and completion, and saline (sodium chloride is salt) and water. In fact, many sea related terms such as sailing and sailor have root in sea salt. The word 'Marine' is a phonetic Mary-ne, a mother goddess.

In alchemical study, [7]Paracelsus claimed salt was the "physical body" remaining after combustion, Effectively Paracelsus claimed that the physical manifestation of life was salt imbued with life energy, when all energy was removed the remnant "salt" was the container for potential primordial polarities in hermetic principle, the *Prima-Materia*. As [8]Pytha goras said "'Salt arises from the purest sources, the Sun and the sea'. And conceiver of metempsychosis, the "transmigration of souls", which claims that every soul is immortal and, upon death, enters into a new body.

This would be a new "vessel", Ve-ss-el.

---

[7] Known as the father of toxicology, Paracelsus (1493 to 24 September 1541), born Theophrastus von Hohenheim was a Swiss physician, alchemist, and astrologer of the German Renaissance.

[8] Pythagoras of Ancient Greece: c. 570 – c. 495 BC was an Ionian Greek philosopher and the eponymous founder of the Pythagoreanism movement.

El is a Mesopotamian word for god, a polytheistic god which is the root of our word "All" which effectively is literally all, the universe, all time, and all its contents. Anything that ends in el describes "all pertaining to" whatever proceeds it. So Ang-el, means all pertaining to Ang, and 'ang'or 'eng' means word, we use in in the word l-ang-uage. And the angels are considered "messengers of the gods".

Gods, at the time were not how we imagine them now, they were classifications of spirit essences that ran through concepts. For example, let's say anything that runs on our modern electricity, would be ruled by the god "electricity", if it creates light, like a light bulb, the hierarchal ruler god would then pair with the light god.

 They did not take form. The only reason they have developed human characteristics is due to art. How do you depict a god?

Hathor

Hathor, believed to also mean house of Horus, takes her name as a mother goddess from the house of Taurus which was the celestial age between 4400bce and 2200bce which in its beginning slightly predates the Egyptian dynastic period but reached its epoch around 3,000bce when Egypt became unified under its capital Memphis, 30 miles south of modern-day Cairo. We don't have much knowledge of that period, but we do know it was a period of great prosperity. We are going back to the first dynasties and pharaohs here at the early formation of the unified Egypt.

Each astrological age is based on the astrological shift of the Sun as we rotate in our galaxy. Our modern zodiac is broken into twelve signs of the 360-degree rotation, giving each sign 30 degrees of our skies. Unfortunately, the constellations don't all fit exactly into each of those 30 degrees perfectly as some are much larger than others. This causes much speculation as to how and when the transition from one age to the next is calculated. But 2,160 years is the most accurate mathematically. If we divide those years by the 30 to get the measurement of one degree of motion, it takes Seventy-two years. Remember that, it will later come back to bizarre effect.

Reducing numbers is simply the method of adding component numbers together to get it reduced to a single number.

For example, the years above 2160 would be reduced by adding 2+1+6+0 which equals nine. Reducing seventy-two would be 7+2 which coincidentally also equals nine. Because of our Moon, every seventy-two-years again coincidentally our Earth shifts on its axis by one degree also, which makes the Sun's position in the ecliptic at the time of the vernal equinox shift against the background of the stars, it is by this we calculate which astrological age we are currently in.

This wobble actually changed what is now our north star Polaris from the North star as observed by our ancestors, and five-thousand-years ago the star mostly aligned with our current north pole was a star called Thuban. At this time, Aldebaran, a red giant star only 65 light years away of the constellation Taurus was aligned with the vernal-equinox where the Sun would rise preceded by the planet Venus.

The word Aldebaran is Arabic and means "The follower" but in Greek, Aldebaran in known as "The Torch Bearer", cross the Atlantic and due to its brightness, ninth brightest star in the sky, it also is a torch bearer as Aldebaran cast light on the seven women in childbirth which is the nearby constellation we know as the Pleiades.

Aldebaran is easy to find if you can find Orion and his three most visible stars of his belt, following the upward tilt, it's the first bright star you see. Bright stars are considered illuminated, and therefore wise, three wise stars traveling from the east following a bright star to the place where a virgin mother was giving birth to the new king. It is quite clear this astrological story, is describing what we would call the nativity. But the one familiar to us, is just one of the repeating cycles of the births of the new aeon, the new age of man which is a time period dictated by an astrological event, no different to how we use the Sun to measure a year, or a day by the Earths rotation in relationship to it.

Simply put, there was not one Jesus, there has been many throughout man's history, with different names.

I tell you all this, to establish exactly where the house of Horus is. Because what that establishes is who Hathor is as a goddess and why she is depicted with bovine qualities. Her principal qualities are the standard feminine qualities, but that which of interest to us is motherhood. The odd thing to note about Hathor is that she was introduced into Egyptian Pantheon by "foreigners" from the land of Punt (pronounced pweny), which has not yet been identified and debate among scholars continues. What we can establish is that Horus, which scholars assume is a sun god, was housed in her at the turn of the equinox into the age of Taurus, making her the holy mother of that age. Yet the more popular family tree in Egyptian mythology places Isis as the mother of Horus. I don't think much as changed over the years, so I'm pretty sure while there can be doubt about who a father is, the mother is rarely in question.

What we have established is that Hathor herself is from the house of Taurus, but not necessarily the constellation itself, which does, however, have seven birthing mothers. The name Pleiades comes from the ancient Greek, "Plein" where we root our words "Plane" similar to "Planets" explained earlier as "wanderers" but, another definition less linked to the planets   plein also means "to sail" linking them to our salt/sea reference. There seems to be a definite connection to the stars as material objects sprinkled like salt in a great sea. Even today we call astrological objects "Bodies" Phonetically Bo-days the bovine supporting the material body view of matter (Germanic: Mutter, means mother) and in Islam the Pleiades cluster is called "Ath-thurayya" which is an undeniable phonetic match to Hathor-raya.

The First Logos.

The visible, the invisible and the indivisible.

The unbound potential of the undivided cell is reflected in the creation of the universe as it is in the creation of mankind. The trinity of Abrahamic religions is the trinity of the parabrhamanic brahma of Hinduism. It is a papered-over concept that this cultural trinity is greatly divided, in truth the unity of the Brahma and Abrahama only reveals itself when these words are written aside each other. 'Ab' means father in Aramaic and Hebrew 'abba' it is the root of the word we may be familiar with in the monastery 'Abbot' which we also call 'fathers', or parent with a masculine designation, Rah, Egyptian simplified sun god, father of the light, the light being his child we know as Horus.

Brahma in his mythology, sprang forth from his golden egg, a concept of creation creating the creator. The golden Egg of the first concept of the universal state which is your potential on a cosmic scale, all you are is a reflection of the greater universe. This golden egg concept equally is symbolic of sun worship and atomic structure, in modern science the egg symbol above is also the astrological symbol for the Sun . What we are considering here is what physicists would call the singularity prior to the big bang, a potential unity of time-space in which all things were unified prior to division. There is only conflict between spirituality and science if you decide that one of them is more suited to your path than the other, however by restricting your discipline to take precedence of one over the other, you restrict your ability to grow objectively.

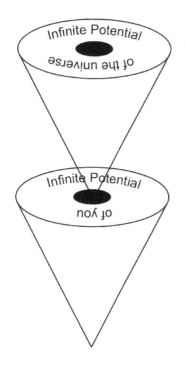

The ability to conceive a singularity can take some consideration, indeed while many claiming to be scientific minded can seemingly express an understanding of it for their argument, they lack the raw presence of what it really means on a spiritual level. For example, it could be argued that the "big bang" never occurred and that we still exist in that singularity, that the big bang is simply a construct of the observation of a consciousness which existed in the singularity created to cater to its need of understanding of its conception. The universe as we experience it, is a singularity in the process of either forming order or forming chaos.

The infinite potential of the self is a microcosm of the infinite potential of the universe in its singularity form and the expression of self is less dependent on physical manifestation than it is of mental manifestation. You are purely consciousness, all elements of you that constitute the physical are on a molecular level disposable and regularly are disposed of and replaced. None of the atoms that compose your body were with you when you were younger. In fact, some of the atoms that make up your body now, possibly belonged to long dead people, plants, stars and planets. Our physical self is simply "not us", we more-so lease the atoms for short periods of time. Our mind changes in its cognitive state of "ego" the present you, and our memories degrade because the atoms that we stored them in have moved on, holding only a simile of their data. Matter itself is the formation of energy into physical resistance to its environment, the singularity dividing. We measure the universe in its division using time and space, yet the third element, consciousness we isolate to individuals, never assuming that what is our consciousness was once a unified consciousness in that singularity, equally dividing and expanding to form independence in the same way matter had.

But what of time? Time, the sequential expression of change in observable epochs, was once unified with this consciousness and matter in its singularity as the first Logos. We perceive it as a linear measurement, which forms part of dimensional measurement of state. But time surely must expand in its dimensions, but we have assumed it has some universal constant, says who? Completely engulfed in the environment of time we cannot measure it objectively. As we age, we often claim time seemingly goes much quicker, again this is subjective rather than objective, we have no external markers to compare since it is a shared, but unique experience. Maybe time is going quicker, in which case we must assume that a counter force to the material expansion of the universe is met with a diminishment of the expression of time.

Returned into the Angelish (English) Language. And the true meaning of the word "PAGAN". You will have been told various etymologies of what "Pagan" is, its roots, its meanings such as country dweller, heathen, it is etymologically claimed to root in Latin from the word "Paganus". Yet as a modern word its definition is ambiguous, and its origins even more so. People familiar with my work will know that I seek to expose falsities in etymology of the English language because the English we speak now barely existed eight hundred years ago unlike most other historic languages of age old cultures. Our language has been fabricated and within it, what we call the "occult" or unseen esoteric meanings have been woven in to hide a secret meaning to fulfil the profess of the language of "Tongues" or the "Angel language", Anglish. The period this came about was known as "The Dark Ages", where the church, primarily spread its word in Latin, but using concepts of philosophy from Greece and theistic principles of the Hebrew and Egyptian pantheons of the Middle-East, or were they?

The Language of the Britons in the land we know as "Great Britain" originally called Albany were primarily a Celtic, Norse Germanic mash of people who adopted many influences, but the name England, or land of the Ings we are taught evolved from the influence of the Anglo's and the Saxons (Anglo-Saxons) as supporting the concept of a natural evolution of the English Language from its neighbouring influences, heavily including the French where we do indeed see many word similarities today. We are told that the name Anglo, was given to the people of the islands by the romans as being the Latin word for the people of the British Islands? The rhetoric almost defies logic in its concept yet is readily accepted. It suggests that the name of the islands, was adopted by the people of the country from the invading force, which seemingly already had a name for them upon discovery? They named "England" as "Anglia" and meant "land of the angels". I find it greatly interesting that the Romans who brought Latin, and it is further claimed, biblical concepts to our shores, should think this was a land of angels. Yet, within the same etymology for the word "Pagan" it is described as a culture of the unkempt, heathens and villager folk, in other words the same unkempt heathen grunts named "Pagan" in its discriminatory explanation lived in a land of angels, whose root definition lies in that of the "Messengers of the Gods". In the further reaches of the Island of Britain than the landing areas of the South East still to this day named "Anglia" was the resisting forces north and west, the romans faced fierce opposition from the indigenous people.

Anybody even beginning to investigate the mythology which accompanies the name 'Lucifer' will not travel far in their research before encountering the story of the "Morning star". This astrological phenomenon has created legend after legend across all mythological pantheons reaching far across each corner of the world, in civilisations which to date, archaeologists have not been able to establish any cross-cultural interaction. The Morning Star is the planet we call Venus, even its current nomination "Venus" is an example of just one of those civilisations reverence to the planet.

The Roman Empire expanded rapidly around the time we accredit to the period in which a man we call Jesus was alleged to have lived. The invading army marched and established its influence along its way north into the continent we know as Europe. Europe was named after Europa, a Greek Goddess who was the mother to King Minos who featured heavily in the latest of my personal, Luciferian philosophy books "Luciferianism EgoSum".

Europa, as Gods often are, is one of the moons of Venus and of course, depending on which side of the fence you sit, the planets were named after gods and goddesses, or the planets were aspects of the language of the gods, open to interpretation and divination in a study which we call today "Astrology", the suffix "logy" that you see in the word "astrology" and used often to denote study in English, travelled with the Romans into French from the Greek and means a "logue", story, an account or a narrative. So, the word Astrology, combined with the word "astro" means the story of the stars and lends itself to all our astrological based mytho-logies.

Culture and language traveling with the Romans; who were previously Pagans having one of the larger pantheons of Gods, was a growing new model of a belief system called "Christianity". Even today, ironically this belief system has its headquarters based in Rome. Of course, these details most of you already know, all I am doing is establishing a pathology which is relevant to the topic as it unfolds. I have intentionally made a point of describing Christianity as a "new model" rather than a "new belief system", as any academic being objective while looking into the history of Christianity can clearly see what appears to be an adoption from earlier Pagan beliefs. Jesus be him a man or not, whether the man existed two-thousand years ago or not is an amalgamation of many concepts which predate that timeline.

Objectively, I will not make a call on this and nobody should. Jesus regardless of the validity of his existence, is an icon of this belief system, and that much is a truth.

Prior to the Jesus icon, the concepts which are fundamental to Christianity all existed. It was only under the banner of Jesus that we now collate this system into what we call our modern interpretation of Christianity, and even that is far from the early Gnostics version.

Jesus would not have been the first to teach "love" for example, he would not have been the first called "messiah" or the first to be the child of a virgin. Being objective and not detracting from anything Jesus is meant to represent, all the concepts of rebirth, life after death, living gods, sons of gods, and mothers of gods all existed in what we now call many a Pagan collective.

It is only when assembled under one umbrella that we then can say that "this is the Christian belief system" or "that is the Hindu belief system", or any other divisive collection of beliefs which form a religion. All belief systems are a set of beliefs that already existed but are then appropriated under a heading and used to identify people who unite under that one banner, and all belief systems and religions have shared concepts as much as they have opposing concepts, middle grounds can always be found between any two organised faith systems.

The Morning star is one of the premier dichotomies of the planet Venus. Which is both morning and evening star. I have covered the reasoning many other times, so I will avoid repeating myself, but if you have not seen this link, please do seek it out in my blogs and books as it is essential in understanding a lot of foundational understanding of the occult. Venus, being Earths closest neighbour and approximately the same size is by every definition seen as a "twin planet" whether in relationship to The Earth, or in its split aspects as Evening and Morning stars. It is the epitome of a dualistic nature. And so, in astrological mythology you can assume that any story which implies siblings which are in opposition are aspects of the Venus-logy. They can be opposed in sex, nature, good and evil.

I have now to, as I often do ask you to start to break down words into their component syllables and phonics, to grasp these concepts correctly and find how the planet Venus and her story is so woven into mythology, history, religion and astrology.

I will start with the "Eve-ning Star", do you recognise that name. Eve, first woman? If you are familiar with EVEn superficial occultism and esoteric interpretation of the Bible rather than the de-facto literalist, you will recognise the aspects of Eve, A mother of humanity, wife to Adam the first male within the classification of what we call humanity. Knowing the target audience of this book, you will no doubt be aware of the story of Lilith, the demonised alleged first wife of Adam.

If we astrologically construct this concept into planets and their observation from our subjective earth view, Eve would be the second wife, Lilith the first; both would be the twin aspects of Venus. Adam could either be the Sun , Mercury or most likely Earth, remember these are twinned pairs, which are opposing. If both females are aspects of Venus and one in the same, they are both at different points in the day paired to Adam. Eve would be representing the "**eve**ning", the restoration of balance, a subjective "good" wife. The "**Eve**-IL", not so charming wife would be El-IL-ETH (Lilith). The astute of you will have noticed that there are some older Mesopotamian gods named there that I don't want to venture into in this work because it opens up all sorts of tangents that you must eventually assemble yourself, I hope I just give you a path to walk along, but EL, EnLIL and Ea have all formed their influence into what we now call English language.

Eve, the evening, comes at night making her the second wife and restoring balance as I suggested, Lilith, the Morning Star is the female version of Lucifer in this story. Many will equate Lilith as being a consort of Lucifer, but that all comes to how you perceive a consort to be. What we have is oppositions to oppositions and oppositions within each of those oppositions ad-infimum. Male to females, being one in the same as symbolised in [9] Éliphas Lévi's Baphomet.

In legend, Lilith was condemned for refusing to lie beneath Adam, this analogy is a mirror of the Lucifer pride story where superiority is displayed by he or she in this case is established by acquiring the position which is highest. Lilith Morning-Star assumes her place over Adam the way Lucifer assumes his place above "God", it's the same story. Thanks to this, Lilith is perfectly suited to be an icon for female equality or opposition to male domination in the same way Lucifer represents mankind's apotheosis aspirations. Lilith

---

[9] Éliphas Lévi Zahed, born Alphonse Louis Constant (February 8, 1810 – May 31, 1875), was a French occult author and ceremonial magician.[1]

and Lucifer are the male and female aspects of Venus. Lilith and Eve are Good and Evil aspects of female Venus, Lucifer and Jesus are the male aspects of Venus, and good and evil are aspects of God (male Adam) and Evil (female Eve/Lilith) God=go-od, Evil=Ev-lil. All are twines interloping to weave the tapestry of life.

However, it is here that these one to one relationships fall over, as they are a trap all too easy to fall into, and we do, creating no end of forums arguing over what some aspect of archetype means. So rather than argue that Lilith and Eve represent Venus, we must understand that Venus as a planet is indeed simply a layer of the metaphor. This is essential learning to your experience as an occultist. If you immerse metaphors and allegories sufficiently as is done with esoteric and hermetic knowledge, you can easily lose yourself in representation.

One could argue, as I have above that Lilith and Eve are the aspects of Venus, and that Venus is Lucifer, and that The mother goddess is The Moon, and that moon means one, or mono an anagram of moon, but then I could continue that mon means man alone. All these arguments have weight, gravitas if you like, but what we need to understand is not that these stories represent celestial objects, or that celestial objects are used to create stories, that's for the sheep to follow. We must concede that the allegories represent divine principles which can be applied to any objects. The raising of The Moon, before the Sun , is as valid as that of Venus. Lilith is more readily associated with The Moon than she is with Venus, and so many historians, theologians will simply say Lilith, is an ancient story telling of The Moon, refusing to lay below Adam (The Sun or maybe The Earth depending on subjective viewpoints in this case). But the truth is Lilith isn't that "body" of celestial presence we call moon, but the nature of the forces which cause The Moon to orbit The Earth, the principles that she does rise above her consort whomever it shall be.

On the Subject of Lilith for devotees to her presence, I would advocate any dedications to her to be held on Halloween, the 31st of October. Not because it's an easy "spooky" cool and edgy date to perform a dedication to a woman so readily demonized, but actually for good reason, incidentally the next full moon on October 31st is in 2020, so If you have opportunity then, there is much to be gained. Although that's a Saturday, if you want to combine that with a moon-day sometime in the future, well you've ticked all the celestial boxes for Lilith dedications.

The October full moon is the completion of The Moon cycle, and the completion of the October cycle. October is Lilith's month. October originally the eighth month, was called "Wynter-Fyllith" the beginning of "fall" as she too fell from grace. But fall is also a word which represents the completion of the cycle, or the beginning of the end, that downward spiral which means her belly is "full", full and fall really are heavily associated. Her belly full, winter-full-lith is old Anglo-Saxon. She retires to incubate her babies ready for the spring where she rises once more as Eve or [10]*Eostur Monath,*

---

[10] *Eostur Monath is the Anglo-saxon name for April.*

Fourth month, c. 1300, aueril, from Old French avril (11c.), from Latin (mensis) Aprilis, second month of the ancient Roman calendar, from a stem of uncertain the Easter moon, the virgin. Wynter is divided into two syllables, *wyn* meaning to desire, and *ter* meaning earth. This is the whore of Babylon if you like, from old-English which demonises Lilith as an aspect. The whorish Lilith creates a desire for the material elements of life. Sex is prevalent for closeness and warmth in the cold winter months. The symbol of Lilith is The Moon above The Cross, which could not be any more obvious as an expression of the feminine moon element placing herself above the spiritual cross, however the cross symbol in esotericism really represents the passage of the Sun rising against the horizon, however it works well under either premise, as all good symbols do, they are applicable to many interpretations. The important thing is the positions of the principles rather than the meat of the subjective elements. Lilith is a derivative from the Hebrew word structure which would be read el-eth, both meaning "god" in different forms however the el is the male spiritual aspect, and eth (earth) the feminine article of the same unified god, effectively the word el-eth simply would extend a wholistic god into its feminine material form. ✝𝒹 is "Eth" written in Hebrew, note the bovine 'bet' addition to the cross "tau" symbol.

I hope these links are beginning to appear to you now in which parables are written as very literal stories, yet on a level intended for esoteric understanding reveal astrological and conceptual cycles which are universal in nature. The

origin and meaning, with month-name suffix -ilis as in Quintilis, Sextilis (the old names of July and August).

I would claim that April or Aprilis, is a dedication to the goddess Apis.The Sacred Cow.

cycle of the planets, the rise and fall and opposing forces vying for domination within that cycle and how one will always compliment the other. I know if this is your first time considering these abstract concepts of wordplay having deeper meaning than the superficial it will come across as nonsense coincidence, but please just keep looking as you study these stories and your understanding of the occult will explode, the best secrets are those that don't appear to be hidden. Trust me, you have no idea how deep this entwines in the English language, English is the key to all the hidden esoteric bible astrology. Even, Good (**Go**ld) and Evil (**Si**lver).

The purpose of that was to show other examples of these oppositions as being the same. Lucifer is the morning star and Jesus is the evening. Lucifer brings the light, and sadly, as the dark ages and the two thousand years of church opposition to man's development in favour of a reliance on all provisioning god has been the light taker, and that role is as important to humanity as the light bearers, remember balance always.

All is a subjective matter. The church, as supporters of Jesus have opposed the scientific and material development of man by placing the emphasis of man's endeavour into faith alone and a trust in God to provide. Even today many spiritually driven communities such as Quakers, Mormons and others will reject the use of man's achievements in the physical realms, in the world of medicine for example devotees will rely on Gods providence on a personal level rather than embracing scientific methods. If you look at the evolution of medicine in the 10th to 18th century, you find science and medicine was condemned as "Devil's work" and "Witchcraft" and the persecution was extreme.

The objective Luciferian while easy to condemn in principle the resultant actions, should be aware of their own subjective take on this. It is easy to condemn "luddites" who seemingly work against man's development. But they may not be wrong in doing this, bear with me. The balance of two opposing forces is the real pace of development, where our spirituality and physicality work briefly in harmonics. An example of this is technology which works equally to our detriment and our improvement tend to evolve side by side, another double helix of opposing forces, within opposing forces. Alongside medicine for example, its research and science at its very cutting edge, also provides chemical warfare technology, viruses are invented as quick as they are eliminated. If the church had not held back man's technological advancement in "knowledge" before we were ready with "wisdom" who knows how much destruction early advancement in warfare would've already wiped out all life on this planet, with some form of nuclear war hundreds of years ago.

Jesus, is the death of Lucifer, Lucifer is the birth of Jesus. Jesus is a symbol of bearing of darkness, Lucifer is the bearer of light. Each are equal and subjectively beneficial to any given situation.

Let me put it like this, if you are on a bicycle. Halfway up a hill….is it better to work hard and cycle up the hill? Or is it better to lift your feet and roll down?

Instantly you may feel that the fun would lie in taking the easy road down the hill. And sure, that's right, but what if your goal is exercise, weight loss, and health? What if you want to see the horizons? The Luciferian must always place himself in an objective centre before deciding the actions.

There will be people who will ride that bike down with absolute conviction they are doing the right thing. There will be people, deriding them and claiming they are wasting their lives on foolish fun, where the real rewards come from arduously cycling against the path of gravity. Both are correct, but unless you are aware that both are correct, and have not to prejudice your choice by not considering all options, then and only then have you made the wrong choice. Free will comes from informed choices because taking action merely on first instinct is not free will, it is conditioning to existing preferred factors disguised as free will. You certainly would feel freer (Freyja)

Freyja is unsurprisingly another one of the incarnations of Lucifer, as a feminine aspect of duality of Venus. Like Venus is a Goddess of Love and fertility, making her morning aspect, birth rather than death, the Alpha to the Omega, her counterpart Óðr (Odin), O is the completion of the cycle, A is the beginning.

The duality of Freyja is exemplified in her stories, she has a chariot pulled by two cats. She divides those who die in battle into two. Freya is associated within her own pantheon with Frigg, but I would draw your attention to Heiðr thrice burned, thrice reborn is also the legend of a three-day cycle. The astrological seventy-two hours I speak often of. The name is shared root with the Greek Helios, Heiðr has a more Germanic name of Gullveig (gold mist) which is describing the dawn light, "gull" meaning Gold and "Veig" sharing its root with the English word "Vague" which is mist and is the effect you get when drunk. Something missed by other scholars who struggle with the Germanic meanings. What we are explaining here is the morning haze, the fog before dawn in which the direct clarity of the day through its sunlight is only hinted at by the indirect light in which Venus rises in the phosphor of the morning.

Freyja, in Old English would be spelled Frigga, but pronounced the same the "G" making a Y sound. "freeyah or frayar" and cognate with "Priya" whose root is shared with "Prior", like "Eve" means before or "Be-Lo-ve" which is a literal definition of Ve (Venus) low in the sky, being the morning. Of course, there is no need to point out the somewhat now depreciated word "frig" (hard G) being an older English word for "Fuck". So, Sexuality, Lust and love are associated with this Goddess. But that is not a debias term for this act, or it wasn't intentionally developed as such. The act of sex is simply a precursor to the act of birth, Eve, Frigg and Frejya are heralds of the coming dawn and the birth of the sky god Sol, which will make them mother goddesses as a natural offshoot of their nature as fertility. Which brings us to Frigg's day "Frige Daeg", Friday or by its Latin name "Veneris", Venus Day.

Of course, I cannot let this link slip, Ven-Eris, Ven I don't need to explain much more at this moment, but of course Eris (roots from Arise or Rise or Risen) is a twin goddess of the Greek pantheon, who represents discordance, or whose counterpart is concordance, the Goddess Harmonia (think Amun Ra, Moon Ra, Moon Light. It's complexity is an understatement. When we introduce Egyptian pantheon and start getting into Horses, Horus, Hours, Horizon, Risen Son and Sun-Set, Seth and Osiris. I've covered them in my books. Harmonia is where we get the root of the English word

Harmony. This is simply Venus wearing one of her masks, harmony must begin with discordance, in the same way Eve restored harmony to Lilith. Ven, incidentally is Latin meaning "come" Ven-nus" means "come the Sun " sun is presented backwards. Which gives us so much more angelic language to work with.

SUNEV (Sun Eve) again, before sun. And Paganism is all about the "Ven-eration" of the Sun as a deity. We can even use the root of the word Pagan "Peganus" backwards to make "sunagap" and "Sun-Agape" where "Agape" is the Greek word for love.

"Peg-Anus" includes Anus, which shares many roots, trying to avoid the vulgar, its actual Latin for "ring" and "Annus" forms part of Annual, which is a yearly event. Pagans will know the essential study of the annual cycle of the Sun as being paramount to their beliefs. The Pagans, knew for a very long time that The Earth revolves in a ring cycle around Sol, the Sun , there is no doubt. What will have happened is that the knowledge and understanding of this fact was as mentioned earlier, wiped from human knowledge by the dark ages and the science counter culture of Christianity.

For "Pag", you will have to bear with me, Pag in origin (Feg'an) from Old English meant, something similar to what we still use it for, to our children, when we tell them to "go and brush your peggies" and the word pegs, is more a verb meaning to fix, lock or hold as in hold your washing up or peg your tent. As a noun it is the object used to fix by insertion, like a tent peg, it digs into the object. A nail would be a peg under this ancient context. But it really means

"Teeth", particularly sharp teeth or fangs, horns or any pointing and fixing tool, your comb would have pegs.

The fangs that eat time, as they cycle the ring could be seen and the great serpent himself, the evil that will always take us to the underworld, time. His fangs are metaphors on multiple levels. As Ouroboros's head eats his tale, showing the annual wheel of the pagan year, where the head represents your perception of this moment in time. The fangs of the Sun should be seen as spokes of the wheel. Each Spoke represents 1 hour, or one aspect of Horus, the horse. The flying horse of course is "Peg-isis" Pegasus whose pathway is along the Equator, and annually is measured by the "Equinoxes" Equine meaning Horse. Fagan, in Celtic means "little Ardent one" which of course is Venus, as Ardent means "burning" or glowing, and so is the smaller of the two rising significant astrological entities in the morning, Venus the mother, followed by her Sun, son.

The orthodox view on the word Pagan remains in doubt, but an explanation I have concluded which is dear to my heart, roots "Pag" in my very own name "Page". In my years of seeking pride in things which were outside of my control, we look into our own heritage and names looking for answers to some of the questions of self. The heraldic titles and origins of names from our lineage often can be frameworks for adopting boasting rights amongst others when the subject of our origins come up. Always we seek authenticity in our roots, as though establishing our ancestor in the ranks of some culture makes us somehow more authentic in our current incarnations.

In briefly researching my surname "Page" which I am fully aware isn't of interest to you, unless you share the name, I hope you will indulge me into the true origins of the name "Pagan".

Page, as well as being a leaf of a book was once in English heritage a boy, who served a knight or a lord; an apprentice if you like. My pride in former days told tales of "knights in training" as a sought to higher nobility to my ancestry than a servant boy. In modern days "page boys" are still features at weddings and customary ceremonies. Trace the name further back and we get to French, then to Latin "Pagina", with a pie root "to fasten" or "to affix", despite this in French it remained "A youthful servant".

What gets interesting is a theme throughout, not of the mixed status of the boy in question, but the state of youth. To page someone is to send a servant to go fetch another. There seems to be three threads running through this name, young, servitude and bearing information. My youth has left me, so I cling to my destination according to name as being a server of knowledge; as the namesake written in this book, each page I hope serves you with at least food for thought.

To an earlier incarnation the pa (male) as in "papa" and "patriarchy" can be traced back to Greek "Padion" and "paidos" which means child. Paidon shares a lot with phonetic semblance to Pagan, or "pagon". It is important to remember that the laws we have governing spelling didn't exist, written word barely existed and so when it comes to exploring roots of words, phonetics in my opinion are more important than any other method, spelling I believe allows you to appreciate geographical influence whereas phonetics hosts truer root functions.

Παιδί-paidí-Child.

Never in my searches of self-pride did I want to pay attention to the servitude and child interpretations of my name. But, if we are children of this mother earth and father spirit, then surely Pagan adopt this more global presence of a product of the universe and of nature. Pagan is commonly claimed to be Latin for "country dweller" yet what is a country dweller, what is a country, but the land. The claim that these people were "rural" in its etymology makes no sense. Why? Because there was no sense of rurality in the aeons from which these words root, we are dismissing huge timelines by claiming there was a great distinction between rural lands and city, when even the largest city would be villages by comparison today, the whole of Rome was merely 7 square miles, which makes it just over 2.6 miles by 2.6 miles, a one hour jog for the average person.

We envisage a country dweller to be some sort of lower-class bumpkin, living in the woods. Yet comparatively two thousand years ago, one could argue where is the alternative? There were no metropolises in the way we envision them today as cities of hustle and bustle. The major civilisation centres were few and far between. The Latin root, no doubt took some influence from the Greek, yet Pagus meant a region of earth, much the same way we use the word "land", but land which can be identified as a region, specifically one which one would consider ones origins to be. These concepts all come together as being children of an earth mother. The "an" or "en" suffix to pag, simply as it still does means

"Made of" or "has the qualities of" and so lends itself to your origins of "from which land do you hale" that theme follows the thread that Pagan means "people of The Earth mother".

This I believe is the true definition of the word "Pagan". Of course you can follow the orthodox etymology, but seek also as much support in evidence of that theory as I have provided with mine.

The Synodic Cycle

The synodic cycle is the period of time taken for one of the planets to return to its original point in relation to two other objects, it sounds complicated I know, but in astrology and in the measurement of the stars and planets relative to our view as we travel through-out the year, we have to consider that space is a three dimensional void, where everything in it is floating around in its own little way. In space, there is no absolute fixed point that we can use for mapping like we do here on earth where we predominantly need to map in two dimensions, like "turn left at the post office". The whole galaxy is a system of wheels within wheels. There are those words again, whole and wheels.

Without those street markers, used in orienteering and such we cannot simply say turn left along a path because there is no path, and so we may use compass bearings or some measure of degrees, like "turn 35 degrees" or commonly written as 35° where the little circle represents the word degree. In space of course, we also have deal with the vertical axis of elevation, and of course elevation is subjective to your current personal orientation, there is no definite up or down, just like on earth there is no absolute left or right, it's all relative to you, at best!

Sitting here on earth, we know that The Earth rotates around the Sun. From our earthbound view and as the ancients understood, it appears as if the Sun follows a circular path around The Earth, but thanks to Copernicus's book *De revolutionibus orbium coelestium* published in 1543, we are told the beliefs of the scientific community until that point favoured [11]Ptolemy's view of the cosmos which believed that the cosmos rotated around Gods favourite planet, the Earth which Ptolemy claimed was the centre of the universe at around the year 150AD. This if course is rubbish, not The Earth centric ideas of Ptolemy, the idea that Copernicus revolutionised man's understanding of the cosmos. The evidence is abundant that ancient man worked on a solar centric system just as we have today. I won't take away Copernicus's credit of this return to the solar centric model. Clearly, we "forgot" or the knowledge was hidden. I'm of the mind to suggest that it was "Hidden" to protect it from the dark ages of man, where science was a forbidden practice, heresy to the powerful roman catholic church responsible for holding back the advancement of mankind for nearly the whole of the two thousand years of the Piscean age.

Placing the Sun as the centre of the solar system has allowed us now to reinterpret the texts such as *The Bible*, not literally as the church has presented for two thousand years, but as a work of occult mastery. Contrary to many scientific minded people's idea of *The Bible,* it is actually a book embroidered with the brilliant minds of ancient scientists who disguised their astrological studies as the stories of the Abrahamic God's pantheon. Simply put, it is not that *The Bible* is stolen Pagan beliefs, although that does lend a hand, the truth is The Bible is a metaphoric study of astrology The Astro-Logos.

---

[11] Claudius Ptolemy (/ˈtɒləmi/; Greek: Κλαύδιος Πτολεμαῖος, Klaúdios Ptolemaîos [kláwdios ptolɛmέːos]; Latin: Claudius Ptolemaeus; c. AD 100 – c. 170) was a Greco-Roman mathematician, astronomer, geographer, astrologer, and poet

Pagan, Christian and all other religious festivals are worship of an astrological system shared across The Earth.

For our *priMary* concern the synodic period is established between two objects, ourselves The Earth and observation point, the Sun , which for our purpose is the fixed point of reference, since we are working on a solar-centric model as Copernicus suggested and the ancients also did, and the object of our interest is the prime goddess, the planet Venus.

These three celestial objects give us the three objects for our synodic (sin(sun)odic(Odin)) study.

The Earth, we know by our regular use of the calendar takes 365 days to return to its starting point passing into the doorway of the new years in the month of the two-faced god of doorways Janus, January. This is known as our orbital period.

Venus also has an orbital period of 225 days and 225 in [12]Ge matria reduces to 9 (2+2+5=9), the word Venus has an English Gematria value of 81 (v=22,e=5,n=14,u=21,s=19) which also reduces to 9 (8+1=9). Nine is a very significant number in the numerology values of Venus.

---

[12] Gematria /gəˈmeɪtriə/ (Hebrew: גמטריא, אירטמיג,□ plural תוארטמג□ or גמטריאות,□ gematriot)[1] originated as an Assyro-Babylonian-Greek system of alphanumeric code or cipher later adopted into Jewish culture that assigns numerical value to a word, name, or phrase in the belief that words or phrases with identical numerical values bear some relation to each other or bear some relation to the number itself as it may apply to Nature, a person's age, the calendar year, or the like. A single word can yield multiple values depending on the system used.

The synodic period is simply the measurement of the relationship where both The Earth and another object align to the same point together. Or as astrologers would say "when they are in conjunction" so a great place to measure from is when The Earth, Venus and the Sun all line up perfectly. The Earth takes 365.5 days to orbit the Sun , we know, but since Venus only takes 225 days there will be another 140.5 days left before The Earth reaches the point where it last aligned to Venus, by then Venus will be three-quarters of its way into its next year. In fact, it will take Seventy-two years before the two planets and the Sun all fall back into a conjunction. Here's where the Gematria starts getting freaky, 7+2=9. "Wow" the ancients thought, "there must be something to this which is not random, but quite mystical, holy and godlike in its architecture."

But it gets a little bit weirder. You see we measure cycles (circles) in degrees, which are the division of a circle into 360° (3+6+0=9), and weirder in those seventy-two years it takes for Venus to scoot by before we reach the original starting point it passes between us and the Sun five times.

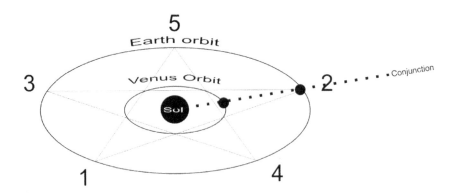

Which gives us our five-sided star, or the pentagram. And of course, because we measure a complete cycle in degrees totalling 360, and we make conjunctions five times in that period. 360/5 gives us the number of degrees in each of those outer angles (Angels), guess what 72°.

Now the fifth letter in the Hebrew alphabet and ours is E (masculine) (in Hebrew pronounced He or Hei). 'He' masculine is a definitive first article for a male and we can make a man female by adding the sin 'S', S-he.

One of the masculine versions of the morning start is Shahar more commonly called "Helel Ben Shahar" which translates to "Son of the Morning". Its counterpart was the evening start "Shalim" The God of the evening.

It is this particular Hebrew name used in Isiah 14:12-15 which when translated into Latin became Lux-Ferre (Light-Ferrier, or light bearer) creating the character "Lucifer". Do not ever be misled, this, despite academic's claims "Lucifer" was never referring to the King of Babylon, I know for certain that is absolute nonsense. But what it is, is the literalist obfuscation of this celestial event. Believing this represents the King of Babylon is no different from taking the rest of the bible literally.

The name Helel is written הילל

Read from left to right is E (he), Yod (y), Lamed (L), Lamed (El). Which can also be pronounced hail, meaning to call.

Helel has a gematria value of 6, it is 9 turned on its head.

Block serif	Block sans-serif	Cursive	Rashi	Phoenician	Paleo-Hebrew	Aramaic
ה	ה	ה	כ	∃	∃	ה

What you may not have associated with He and She is adding another predominantly feminine letter, the Tet. 'The' the most glorious word in our language, a determiner and absolute definite article, meaning we are referring to something specific rather than a generalisation "get me THE bottle" rather than "get me A bottle" and source of the word "Theology", which means either 'the word', 'the logging', or 'the study' of god/s. If you are an Atheist, the A at the beginning means Against, Anti or opposing. The Alpha opposes the Omega. A-Theist, opposes the principle of a "theo" or God.

The O, the omega. Which means "Big O" from Greek, or the concept of a whole being all or everything, the "big everything" being the universe or whatever is beyond, the study of what was once the singularity. Since concepts of god were historically the universe as a pantheism, being atheist actually would mean you didn't believe in the universe as a single "The" and so you would probably be opposed to science of the day. Weird how things have inverted. The Paleo Hebraic symbol much more closely resembles our English 'E' but backwards and to me the three horizontal lines represent the three celestial objects, while the vertical line represents the conjunction. Making four elements to the fifth letter, (4+5=9).

But maybe in the context of a more localised study of the heavens, 'the big O' refers only to the seventy-two-year synodic cycle of Venus, rather than the universal concept of all things, "as below, so above". The planet Venus is never more than 47° from the Sun from our earthly view, and although we picture the objective view of our solar system on a horizontal (Horus-ontal, of the horizon) plane, such as we see in my diagram below, the way we experience it from earth is vertical (ve-rticle).

From our view it's a little more like this:-

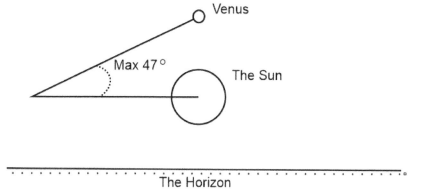

While Venus is ahead of the Sun , making it the morning star, it is known as an inferior conjunction where THE article which is inferior, is the Sun . The morning star has rebelled against "THE" sun, claiming her throne in heaven.

Because Venus is closer to the Sun , we know that the gravity of the Sun keeps Venus close to it, but in ancient mythology, Venus was the bearer of the light, and so pulled the Sun across the sky in the same way an ox would pull a cart.

The Ox, Symbol represents the whole cycle and the axis. The vertical and horizontal. We still use today in all sorts of dimensional measurements like compasses, watches.

For those of you who have a passion for the Nordic pantheon consider this. The reading of events can be attributed to Urðr as being The Earth and can be spelled "Urth" which is your fate, where your "feet" are. Our modern interpretation of fete may seem like the future or destiny, but that's a modern misuse, as you see fete although it may seem like future (foot-Earth) is actually "written in stone" it is unchangeable and so represents a metaphysical past of the uninvolved self. In which your path (or feet) cannot change course in the physical self, however, the spiritual-self's evolution from the learning of that path is not fixed.

Verðandi, Venus is the concept of time our original Chronos and is presented in Norse as the "now" or happening, the conscious you in balance with the heavens and The Earth.

Now "Vero" in Italian, means "real" or true, from the Latin "Verus."

And finally, the triad is completed with of course the Sun representing the heavens, or the head, Skuld (skull) Which is where you will go, or what you attain so is associated with the future. In Norse Mythology these are called the Norns. The transformation from the physical to the spiritual is represented in the Poetic Edda which includes the *Tree of life* in its reference.

Thence come maidens
much knowing
three from the hall
which under that tree stands;
Urd hight the one,
the second **Verdandi**,
on a tablet they graved,
Skuld the third;
Laws they established,
life allotted
to the sons of men,
destinies pronounced.

These three Goddesses in Norse mythology reside below the Giant tree Yggdrasil and were charged with the fate of humanity. Urd (Urðr) represents is the maiden at our feet, The Earth, the world (wyrd). In Abrahamic we can relate here to the story of yet another "Mary" who isn't Mary of Magdalene (but is really) She is Mary the sister of Lazarus, because all these Marys are Allegories for the Mother Goddess.

In the story of the *Anointing of Jesus*, Mary the sister of Martha and Lazarus featured in three of the four Gospels under her name of Mary, and in the fourth she goes unnamed, this is the book of Luke where she is simply referred to as the sinful woman. Sin is the downward fall of virtues of the sin-wave which makes our wholistic and universal vibration. The allegory in this tale features patriarchal supremacy in the hidden and encrypted layers. When this Mary places her head at the feet, it conveys several hidden esoteric messages. Some manufactured by the church, some hidden in that superficial meaning.

On the surface the tale begins insinuating that the female is subservient to the male in the patriarchal view which the church was fond to promote in the 15th century. Temptress whores were like demons to the puritanical mind, woman is portrayed as sinful, yet redeemable. By leaving her in this context it became much easier to promote the misogynistic agenda to the uneducated masses. In the deeper subtext, the individual is divided into three aspects previously described, spirit, body and the offspring of the two which makes the whole. The spirit, our mind is to be considered superior to our body, since the mind should be master of our physical desires, temptation is seen as sins of the flesh. Mary, by placing her head and uppermost part of the body-physical at the feet of is symbolic of the master of the flesh in a spectrum. Jesus here is not the son of god personified, but a representation of us. We are all Jesus, a child of the father and mother gods and you stand on the head of the mother Goddess, earth below, heavens above. Mary's head below upon Jesus's feet is an allegory misunderstood and can be read as derogatory to women, submissive. But could also be a geographical map of the spectrum of physicality or rather the elemental alchemy hierarchy, as Mary represents The Earth, our feet touching The Earth and waters as she washes his feet, the lower elements, Jesus representing the higher elements of air and fire.

Shakespeare made use of them as the old crones or "Weird Sisters" in the 15th Century play Macbeth, which also feature in Greek mythology as "The Fates". The word wyrd (note the phonetic links between word and wyrd(weird) which is an Anglo Saxon Norse origin which describes the tapestry of life, as an interwoven mesh of events such as described by the "word of God" if it was to be read as an astrological book. As a physical substance the written part of the tapestry is manifest word, world. As its substance it complies with The Earth part of the triad, [13]Wold, the old unchangeable, and the roots of the tree which resides in the ground. "Would" another metaphoric branch of this family of phonetic roots, more strikingly resembles the term for fate, as it Transends past and future in its tense, "would" hints at changing fate that cannot be changed, as in past tense "What would I have done?" or predictive future "What would be better?". The "Wo" often repeated I have previously said links the feminine, wo-man element. Although the very masculine Odin (woden) fits with this concept. Described as the very Abrahamic sounding "All Father"; like Venus, Odin is supreme god of war and poetry and knowledge and wisdom.

The actions we take as manifest beings, translate as three components of the self. Represented as The Earth which is our bodies and our past, Venus represents our ego, heart and presence; and our minds, the crown, corona future self, which is representative of pure spirit, Sol, Sun and Soul.

In understanding the ancestral universe, we must dismiss modern ideas of creation and embrace a simpler and more rounded view of life as it presents itself not just in ourselves but on a grander universal scale. A fundamental understanding of life comes from observation of the cyclic

---

[13] Wold is an Old English term for a forest or an area of woodland on high ground; it is cognate with the Dutch word woud and with the German word Wald, as well as low German Wohld, all meaning forest. It became weald in West Saxon and Kentish.

universe and humankinds place in that cycle must therefore be considered a cycle. The days and nights turn into weeks, months and seasons and all things were measured in such ways.

To begin with, life itself begins as mother. We are physically integrated into mother regardless of our eventual sex denomination. We are all women as we are an integral part of that physical unit. This essence of motherness is carried with us as a spiritual archetype descending through history; the mother will always be who we are as a species to expand on the gnostic principle which I have already covered. Now let's align those principles to a more physical and less esoteric approach while explaining them in the way's modernity has forgotten. These principles are still evident in ancient writings when we change the way we read them, rather than try to contextualise ancient thought into a modern context; we must change our current setting into an ancient mindset.

What many would call secret histories, can often be mistaken for merely forgotten theories and philosophies, or science of our ancestors rather than implying that there was some malintent cover up of secret knowledge.

In modern day science, we describe this as distant biology which we abstract from the fundamental sense of identity with characters such as XX [14]chromosomes eventually

---

[14] The XY sex-determination system is the sex-determination system found in humans, most other mammals, some insects (Drosophila), some snakes, and some plants (Ginkgo). In this system, the sex of an individual is determined by a pair of sex chromosomes. Females typically have two of the same kind of sex chromosome (XX), and are called the homogametic sex. Males typically have

becoming the XY chromosomes. It's all very clinical and allows our egotistical modern mores to credit us with being more knowledgeable about the matter than our predecessors. But that's simply not true, they were well aware, even without the medical books, developments and microscopes to back it up. The way they presented it, lost in what we could call religious artefacts, should not be considered the case that they didn't really understand the biological principles, more that we don't understand their way of presenting this knowledge.

The cycle of life we can simply understand in its most simple form can be represented as such

This image above is the basic idea of an instance of a person's life. We began "mother", in mother, as mother, without reason, knowledge or awareness. This mother-self was more than just our instance, it was our mother-self going back through all our maternal generations. We really need to consider this mother self being a greater than ourselves concept, in the same way we embrace the father god characters as eternal aspects or entities, so is the mother

---

two different kinds of sex chromosomes (XY), and are called the heterogametic sex.

goddess we are physically a part of expressing herself in every one of us.

We were innocent as in the garden of Eden. And what you must also remember is that the mother goddess is imbued within us outside of time. That means that simply being unaware we existed, wasn't considered non-existence. The maternal aspect of ourselves existed long before our physical gestation, she exists as the mother goddess. And so this is their expression of us all being a XX chromosome, not only does the biology support this modern understanding, the physics do to when we use expressions like "we are stardust" and scientist show that we are made from the very same atoms that came into existence and created the stars at the dawn of time. These are all expressions of the mother "us".

This simple diagram above shows the passage of our lives as we transition from the mother(physical), into the father (spiritual) self.

As we attract more atoms and grow physically in substance, we also grow spiritually and insubstantially into more reason, as we establish who we are from a purely mental perspective. In the passage of time, we head more towards the father state of existence, or rather nonexistence in a physical sense, otherwise known as death, the doorway.

The principle, as all universal principles should be, is a fractal, and so anything that applies to the microcosmic sense can be applied on a larger scale.

And so, to turn this linear principle into a cyclic one, we introduce more complex elements.

Such as our manifestation of both spirit and substance as a result of the sexual union of the two archetypes of feminine and masculine via the physical manifestations of a previous union, our own mothers, and fathers. The resultant child offspring is a microcosm within that macrocosm which will begin an expression as a new life such as yourself.

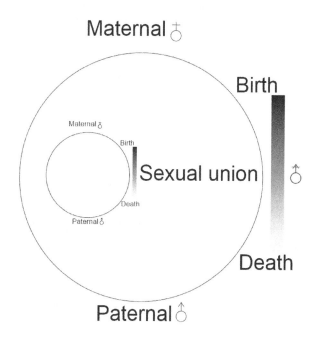

Eve often overlooked in the left hand path in favour of the more brazen and mysterious Lilith, is also a true representation herself of the microcosmic the garden of Eden, she represents the purest and uncorrupted state of manifestation before the fall. In terms that once a woman "knows" a man, then she has condemned herself in the Christian sense, and sadly for Eve, she seems to get her back turned on her not only by the Abrahamic faiths but the left hand path philosophies too, as she's simply not considered edgy enough. But as pre-presentation of the mother goddess, there is none higher, mother of humanity, bearing the burden of the first child and the punishment of the jealous Jehovah. Eve did not tempt Adam with a fruit, she was the fruit which made the serpent rise. She was the first Lucifer, not the snake as she disobeyed the Abrahamic god and dismissed his authority while presenting enlightenment from the tree of knowledge of the garden.

Much like the two faces of Venus in her aspects as morning and evening-star, Eve becomes more masculine as the Eve'ning star. The evening as a word means to harmonise, to even out and bring the cycle to a close. The story of Adam and eve is the same story of the rise and fall of Lucifer, the garden of Eden is the separated states of the male and female aspects, once unified in sexual congress paradise is lost.

It is only by corruption that Eve is replaced has Lilith to maintain the purity of the feminine in Abrahamic mother goddesses. Lilith who would not lie below Adam is the same metaphor as Lucifer ascending above Jehovah, or Venus rising before the Sun in astrology.

Eve comes before the child. And so Eve's holy day should be more embraced by adherents to the feminine archetype. Her day is "Christmas Eve."

But may be celebrated each evening as she completes her cycle of the day. Lilith, the first wife, is the morning star which brings the light. Or "bears" the light like a mother, Lucifer is in fact, female as a morning star, and progresses into masculinity or int her death and sacrifice as a mother when the masculine energies are introduced into her.

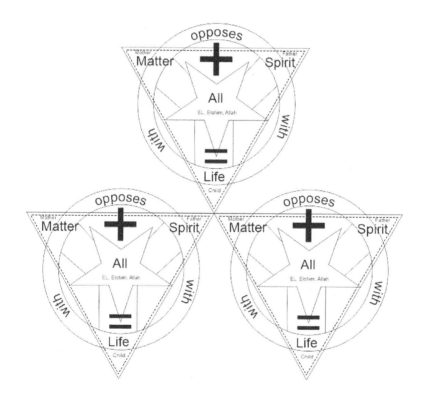

Dedication

Within me is the goddess, for I and she are one, we are one, all are one as nature and world womb.

We are all that has been and all that will ever be, I am the hands of the goddess in that I may shape the world around me and lift that which has fallen as my child. Lovingly I take it into my bosom and nurture it till it may stand as strongly as I do, and I shall lead by example.

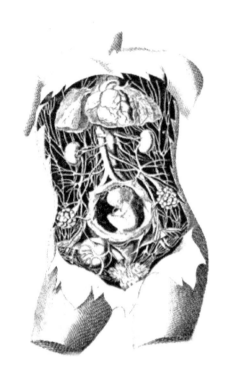

I shall teach it the wisdom of love and nurture of compassion from which every seed may grow in my nature.

I do all this in the essence and beauty of all that is woman, and I shall continue forever to shape this green earth as the present and apparent god and mother.

I am the heart of The Earth, from which all stars are made, I am the lungs of the air and breath from which all wisdom is spoken. I am the mother from which all life flows.

The Prima Materia

The Prima Materia in alchemy is a Latin translation meaning "the first substance". In goddess sense we would know her as "the Prima Madonna" or the first mother, similar in nature to the goddess Hathor mentioned earlier.

As all "MA" and "MO" prefixes are feminine aspects. Madame, Mater, Matter, Mother, Miss, Mary, Marry, Marriage, Matron, Mazda and of course Mass. The word Mastery is the Majestic, initially study of the astrology from the word Astra meaning star and significantly our major star 'The Sun'. There are many a Goddess which follows this formula, and by now you should be able to formulate your own relationships to personal favourite icons of the mother, divine feminine or goddess archetypes and where you should be able to see the origins of these mother goddesses leap off the page whenever you encounter them in our language.

One that goes way back to [15]Sumerian is Ahura Mazda, the creator and sole God of Zoroastrianism system. Zoroastrianism is one of the oldest religious systems we know of and thought, well in my opinion quite clearly one of the root belief systems which has maintained a presence or evolved into our current Abrahamic and other astrological belief systems. In fact, we get the word "Zodiac" from a zoologically based division of the night sky. I'll pull no punches, Jesus and his twelve disciples are nothing more than

---

[15] The earliest known civilization in the historical region of southern Mesopotamia,

another fable such as Arthur and his twelve knights, seated at the round table which describes the solar rotation. Fantasy mythologies used to carry the messages that can be read from the skies. What I will say though, is that doesn't mean that it doesn't make "Jesus", "Horus", "Thor", "Hathor", "Arthur" as they have previously been known any less significant if you consider the universe as being an outer extension of yourself in the holistic (wholly) sense, our current existence extends beyond the material form into a shared self, known as the soul which I will expand upon later in this chapter. These names are merely facades of a concept, the religions which extend their influence under "names" is simply a way of expressing the concept.

Consider this, if we are fractals of an infinite universe. Then we become by definition a greater universe to a smaller fractal; 'as above so below'. When we have an ailment, our nervous system acts on our behalf to try to ratify that ailment. There are lines of communication between us, and the transient atoms that make up our body. Atoms have a relationship with the component parts of their makeup, the Nucleus and its orbiting electrons. The 'as above so below' is the cosmological expression of that where the Sun is such a nucleus.

We are simply atoms, on an atom, orbiting an atom, which orbits another atom and so on. We, the universe and all things are one infinite biosphere. If you want to call belief system and its patron Jesus, Shiva or Ahura Mazda, that's fine. It's just a name. The "secret doctrine" as the theosophist used to call it, is simply the realisation that whatever religion you follow, it stems from the same source concepts of divinity as all the rest. Ahura Mazda is unsurprisingly the highest patron in the Zoroastrian system and means "Wisdom". "Mazda" is Proto-Iranian Mazdāh (feminine noun).

The Prima Donna, or first lady, also Prima Madonna would be first mother, In Christian pantheon, we know her as Mary. In the New Testament Mary is also present at the Birth as the *virgin Heifer* of the new sun god, but also as the whore, in dynamic opposition at his death in the garden of Gethsemane, Mary of Magdalena, also known like in all the pantheons as his wife or mother, or the goddess IsisDonai and Dianna are al derivatives of the mother goddess Inanna). All these goddesses represent a concept of material energy, which is the feminine divine. The feminine aspect, matter is gravitas, it pulls. The male is resistance; it is push.

Mass as I have explained is all material artefacts and all things with physical substance in the universe. And so this feminine aspect of forces express themselves with gravity, or toward the matter, to the grave, male represents birth, not to be confused with the person giving birth, but the resultant birth the outward forces. The male aspect opposes gravity, is considered an ascension and pushes away, opposing the nature of the feminine gravity. The cosmic magic which forms the assembly of atoms within the womb are a feminine aspect of attraction which shows the mother attraction energies to be the most physically expressive and powerful magic in the universe which is observable, male energies like the father god, go more or less without objective product.

Symbolic of these expressions we could use the humble tree whose roots seep into the ground for nurture, nourishment and the feminine succour, the warm, welcoming grave which lies underground. In contrast, the male aspect which sheds seed, reaches for the spiritual light above ground, resisting gravity and creating new life.

Similar to the Ancient interpretations of the tree of life, features of the tree can be considered that the feminine element is an inward attraction, so Mother-Earth and her goddess attractions is responsible for the drawing out of roots of the tree. The trees foundation is literally rooted in the mother as a child within her womb, the male head is naturally expressed by coming out of the ground headfirst drawing ourselves away from the grave or womb, towards the father.

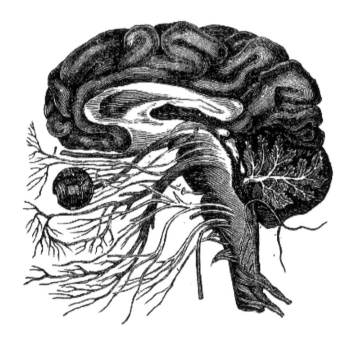

The tree of life, the mother, physical manifestation of human roots in the material plane as represented by the nervous system. The Tree of Knowledge was its male counterpart.

The nourishing soils draw the tree which represents each of us as individuals underground towards her grave. Gravitas, the Latin word for "serious", weight and heaviness is here to be considered that feminine attraction force. The mother is present at both birth and death as we return to our physical grave, this is why in the bible the two significant women in Jesus's life were Mary the Virgin, and Mary the whore, one present at the birth, both present at the death both sharing the name "Mary". The Grave is the domain of the mother, as is her womb, which was also represented in Gethsemane by the tomb in which Jesus was placed. This fear of death, fear of the grave, the contribution of opposing directions towards the aspiring heavens or the cold dark grave of decay created the imagery of both Heaven and Hell and is a major contributor to the demonization of the mother Goddess under this method of allegorizing the concept. The common place of the goddess within western civilization must be forgiven for allowing the allegory of something as wonderful as attraction and gravity which without which we could not experience life on the physical planes, to turn into something perceived as negative.

This transition from growth out of the mother from the cradle to the grave is an observation of Venus from its rise and "rise-istance" away from the observed eastern horizon. Note that Stern (eastern-western) and Birth are all naval or navigational terms relating to a lateral or horizontal plane of The Earth's rotation as the morning star, the male aspect and the son of god, Adam. So, while the morning star Venus is male in the morning, and female in the evening, Adam (atom) and Eve. Because Venus is a representation of a hermaphrodite, and why Venus is known as the other

God/Goddess Aphrodite, who isn't female, but both genders. And Hermaphrodite is the "secret" "Herm" meaning sealed, once of the great secrets of Hermetic wisdom. Let me make it clear the concept of the hermetic. This bi-gender expression is simply again an allegorical way of placing one thing within another, hermetically sealed, like the word "occult" means to hide, to place under the seven seals. The potential of man is light (knowledge) held within matter (wisdom). As the collection of knowledge allows for the application of wisdom, which really is collective knowledge or experience of multiple possibilities which provide the ability to choose the knowledge that is most applicable from a wider reservoir of experience. And so the feminine as container for all knowledge, is the goddess of wisdom under most pantheons.

This very crude diagram below shows how knowledge is identified as separate to the "Dom" or domain of wise. Wise, like "Vis" is rotted in vista, or view. But we are talking about hermetically sealed knowledge, and that is the collection of knowledge within the individual. Your "Image-nation". The knowledge or experience of a certain truth, fact or moment is attracted into your sealed wisdom, to be recalled when needed, indeed the more knowledge we can harvest as individuals the more likely we are to make wise decisions.

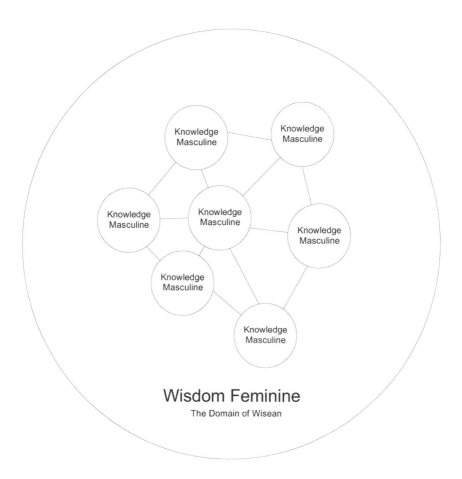

It is this gravitational pull, which makes us driven people to garner knowledge and become better people. This trait, this science, the medicine, this knowledge took us away from the provisions and reliance on the Patriarchal god benefactor god upon whom we should be fully dependent, instead of independent as the mother goddess, who is equal yet opposite.

I realise you may be questioning why earlier I would call Adam the son of god because of traditionalism; we are taught that Adam was the first man. Well, this is just again the literalist rhetoric supported by the church.

But what is Adam if not the first creation of a universal godhead concept, a child is an appropriate categorisation. And since the morning conceptually begins before evening, eve came second. Although hidden within Hermetic secrets is the knowledge of the eternal cycle, where Eve is created before Adam in an infinitely repeating cycle, which is why Adam is born in mourning (morning) the death of the cycle, repeats ad-infinitum.

What later "fell" out of the passage of time was the evening, a second child which was made from the original creation which instantaneous, the two aspects of Venus are one in the same.

The church would say created from Adam's rib, but as a metaphor for Venus, Eve is the second aspect of Venus in her demise towards the grave and the western VVE-ST-ern HORUSion. Eve was never a mere part of Adam; Eve was Adam and the garden in unity as the garden and "Adam & Eve" are representative of the states of us as a divine concept, she represented the demise of Adam also sometimes referred to as the fall of man and the corruption of Adam and the fall from grace to grave.

It is here we need suspend our understanding of all these feminine alignments with negativity in our understanding of what negativity is. Negativity is an attractive force; positivity is a repulsion.

But to see that negative forces are essential to the whole, and that negative forces create as much good and positive forces when thought of as an expression of the use of energy. Pull or push, the forces are harmonic as a whole. It is as important to rest as it is to exercise, it is as important for the Sun to set, as it is to rise. It is only in the harmony of these to forces that two become one which becomes whole. It's a bit like spending money, spending money depletes your resources, yet the purpose of money is to be spent, which then provides you with what you truly need.

Shifting focus back to the soul this chapter opened with. We all The Earths inhabitants and extending further into our solar system share one soul. The Atum, or atom of the Sun , which remember the atom is not just its nucleus, but the sum of its sphere of influence over its orbiting protons which make up the atom as a collective, cosmically it is the whole solar system. the Sun 's atomic-sphere is our shared soul. In modern times and for many lost years the soul has been misrepresented. We are led to believe we each have an individual soul, but that is not the case. The soul is made up of the shared light of the Sun , and the hermetically sealed secret knowledge that the soul is the whole effect that the Sun has on all "bodies" within its influence which includes its masculine-light and feminine-gravity. Simply, what is known in scientific terms as our "solar system" where solar was for the Egyptians the soul of Rah. And the extent of its effect is its Ra-deus (which literally translates to the God-Ra). Of course the masculine has a female counterpart we call diameter, which I hope you can now read as 'Diana mother' which represents the attractive force in-ward bound energies and despite my crossing pantheons, it is where the Sun light of Rah, is attracted to the whole of the sky as it would be perceived in an earth-centric idea that what we call our sky was a feminine aspect which was thought to extended from The Earth.

Dium as in "radium" apart from being a chemical element with the symbol Ra and atomic number 88 in our modern world, is the sky feminine force dium from the matter attracting the Ra father, or Dius which means light.

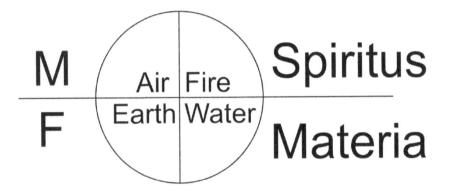

Not to be confused with the air, which is male (heir), the ancients were fully aware that the spherical feminine earth attracted the male air in its "atom-o-sphere", and is bound to the elemental earth mothers which is water and earth.

I promised hermetic secrets in this book, so here is one such example. What will come to pass is that scientist who are always late to the table will discover…you heard it here first!

An example of Mary being the original goddess, the goddess was adopted into the Christian teachings. An example of this alignment to the pre-Christian god, at the last supper the symbolism is divided between the body of Christ and the blood. The body actually represents the material mother goddess. Mary of Bethlem is where Bethlehem is translated from Hebrew into "House of Bread"¬ "Beit Elchem" as the virgin Mary is from the constellation Virgo the virgin. Who in depiction carries a wheatsheaf. The body of Christ is to be consumed, Here the body is a bread-based foodstuff. The Sacramental bread of the Eucharist (giving, charity) one of the seven sacraments in the church.

When Jesus says this is my body, he is referring to the Pagan mother goddess as represented by the Virgin Mary. In turn the virgin Mary, represents the potential Ain Soph, the womb of creation of all things whose primordial essence is pure and untainted by spirit. The blood is the suffering presented by spirit, on a philosophical level, the blood is spilled by the masculine in both the acts of intercourse with the virgin and in conflict. It is these otherwise uncorrelated aspects where the Goddess is often represented as "Love and War". It is not that the divine mother should be considered a pragmatist of love and war, but the target and bearer of the actions. In love she bears fruit, in war she bears the pain.

"LIGHT is the OPPOSITE force of GRAVITY"

As indicated in my description of the divine elements of humanity, the gravitational attraction force is feminine, the aspiring push force of light eternally emanating away from its source is masculine, between are a spectrum of states of that force. This is a hermetic truth always known, and once scientists pick up on this, they will then be able to take us to the next level of human scientific research. Light and gravity are the polar opposite expression of the whole, gravity will be found to be an expression of light in its lowest wavelength.

This secret has alluded us for centuries but was always known by the ancients and is the solution to the building of incredible and impossible structures like the pyramids, they lifted heavy objects using light or transmuting matter into light, and the reason why when things have a high mass they are "heavy" or "heavenly bodies" and when they do not they are considered to be "light". The less mass we have, the more light we have, it is a spectrum of expression and a universal law. We can take it further, when we breath in, the outer soul, or atmosphere is inspiration, and when the father "soul" enters the body of matter, we inspire, in other words, we create the spirit within matter. and so spirit is our individual soul, isolated from the solar soul and when we "ex-spire" expire or die, the spirit leaves the body and returns to the collective soul.

The Sun god Atum, is a cosmic atom, the ancients were fully aware of atoms! And biblical phrases such as "the light of The Earth" did not as it immediately seems refer to the male Jesus, but a hermaphroditic concept of the divine feminine too. The expression is inclusive of The Earth or mother character.

Androgynous Salvator Mundi by Leonardo Di Vinci
bearing the atmos-sphere while holding a binary hand gensture

Rhea

What we are frequently finding is that these gender traits that we have applied to the gods, often interchange. When we seek a truly gender specific deity to represent our gender, like humans, we find the gods are complex arrangements of female and male gender aspects. Rhea, of the Greek pantheon came into her own expression it would seem around 400BCE. Rhea is a great example of how these genders may interchange between cultures. I have often referenced the Egyptian god Ra, as being the god of "light" and the root of our word "ray" denoting that he wasn't the Sun per-se, but instead the eminence of light which is the life-giving father of The Earth. Yet, maybe light was too much of a specific attribute I was trying to conject into my principles. It certainly fit at the time. Rhea, which also is phonetically aligned to the Egyptian Ra (Rea), isn't male (spirit, ethereal) at all, she is very much the mother of all mothers. Rhea is ('Ρέα) metathesis from ἔρα which is consistent with the very maternal-material "ground", but the orthodox scholars argue amongst each other that the true meaning is "Flow" from the Greek ῥέω (rheo) meaning "flow".

When we look at both arguments in their feminine context, there is an alignment between both. And, if I have misinterpreted earlier in my studies the context of Ra, meaning the light itself, it would seem that Ra, Rah, Ray is not male because it is ethereal and therefore masculine, but it is the flow of energies expressed in motion, Ra is not "ray" in the masculine beam sense, but much more obviously "ra-dial", circular in its emanations, feminine like the waves of water and Rhea is a flow of power emanating in the feminine wave form. Chronos, was Rhea's consort so the Pantheon is syncretic with the Egyptian pantheon as like the combination Sun God "Amun-Rah" Chronos is iconic of both the Sun itself, and the passage of time. the Sun from Earth's point of view is the king of the heavens, and also the measure of our days. Chron (crown, crone, corona, chord). In the mythology Chronos is known for eating his children, this clearly is the metaphor for how time is the great destroyer, opposing Rhea's motherly creativity. Until their only surviving and last child Zeus, Chronos had eaten all their previous offspring Hestia, Demeter, Hera, Hades, and Poseidon. Each one of them representing a force or element which is extinguished by time. Zeus however provides the hope of Eternal life, hidden from Chronos in a cave in the mountain, Rhea gave Chronos a rock swaddled in cloth which he instantly devoured believing it to be his son Zeus and so Zeus became one of the many expressions of a very well-known story of a son of the king of heaven, being hidden in a cave, believed to be dead yet returns with the promise of eternal life, Jah (the Rastafarian name of God) or Yiós (the Greek word for son), Jesus (Jah-Zeus).

If we combine the elemental 'Ma' of mother and the queen of all mothers "Rhea" we get the name Ma-ria (Mary). So, what we need to realise is that the *New Testament* accounts of the modern god pantheons the world is holding onto at the moment, much more than the well-reported holidays and festivals, in fact the Jesus story entirely is just a re-hash of a plethora of pantheons which have all expressed the same stories in different ways and have been stolen by modern day Christians as an absolute literal description of events two thousand years ago, but they are much older and are a body of stolen pagan concepts that they are too narrow minded to and indoctrinated into a catholic church version of ancient science and astrology to accept the previous incarnations of the same story. Even in the bible itself Moses is described as a baby, swaddled; being hidden from a masculine king, Jesus is hidden by his followers, as Rhea hides Zeus from Chronos (chroNUS).

If you look up the simplest definitions of name, even in baby naming books Maria reads as:

Latin form of Mary, which is derived from the Hebrew Miryām, a name of debated meaning.

Many believe it to mean "sea of bitterness" or "sea of sorrow." However, some sources cite the alternative definitions of "rebellion," "wished-for child," and "mistress or lady of the sea." The name is borne in the Bible by the mother of Jesus, the son of God. But as mother of the sea she can claim most majesty, often depicted in blue, the colour of the ocean she brings a serenity which is truly the epitome of all goddesses. Even though she has been adopted into the Christian doctrine we are fools if we turn our backs on this divine mother.

Again, the orthodox scholars are squabbling over a word meaning are missing the esoteric concept which when looked at holistically in hundreds of ancient documents, become obvious to the opened mind. "Sea of Bitterness" and "Sea of Sorrow" is almost as though written by literary geniuses such as Wilde to describe the monthly "flow", where as "wished for child" is almost too sad to express when one aligns this to the consequences of a miscarriage, all three are clearly the same thing, a description of the womanly cycle, which is a symbol of failed crop, so to speak.

Rhea in her depiction is flanked by two lions which sit loyally by her side, I believe the lions, are the red mist of dusk and of dawn, in this case the mother goddess is not Venus, but Venus is her lions.

Cybele

The Minoan Rhea's counterpart more readily adopted into the Roman pantheon and prototype to the Virgin Mary in the often-overlooked Turkish mythology otherwise known as the Anatolians was called Cybele. Cybele the Great-Mother Goddess, according to legend spurred the advances of Zeus in favour of a mortal shepherd called Attis. Zeus, not being someone easily rejected "spilled his seed" on her while she slept, the goddess then gave birth to a hermaphrodite demon named

Anatolian incidentally means "Sun Rise" as it represents the land to the east since Turkey is such a large country that extends right across to the Asian (a-zion) continent it finds itself as the land which lies mother to the risen son. Cybele's origins trace her back to the Neolithic Çatalhöyük people who were Asian.

To provide some further metathesis links that might inspire you, the east where the Sun rises, is the birth of a new son (sun), rising from The Earth mother, *Annatto* is also known as *Achiote* is a deep orange colour dye, somewhat like what is seen at sunrise and sunset, one could almost call it "rust" coloured. Zion (ion, iron and lion). Anatolian also translates therefore to The Red Lion, commonly associated to James I, VI of Scotland responsible for the first English translation of the Bible, known as the KJV.

Early representations of Cybel seemingly circulated around a mysterious *black stone* which embraces the feminine concept on two levels, opposing the white light of spiritual patriarchy and stone itself, manifesting the physical earth element.

Cybel would protect the Pergamum people from the showers of stones which fell from the skies. As first mother and mother of gods, her consort was Papas, which should be very familiar to most of us as a almost universal name for "father", and in Greek the word means "Priest", again often ordained priests will be referred to as father. Cybele's Greek title Meter Theon, Meter (μητέρα meaning Mother (Theon (of Gods)), supporting the measured aspect of the female principle which is essential to our understanding, none more so than in the Greek goddess Demeter.

Although seemingly very Pagan in her origins, Cybele easily transitioned into Christian mythology under the premise of being *The Black Virgin* and is still venerated as a mother goddess akin to the Virgin Mary. She was the first Near-Eastern goddess to be adopted by Rome who were sacrificing bulls to her since the second Punic War, 218-201 B.C.well in to the 5th century AD, where it flourished under the Gallic-Gauls, and indeed she can still be found in more obscure churches as a patron *The Black Virgin* which has been assimilated into a regional interpretation of Mother Mary. The significant esoteric meaning hidden in the representation of Cybele is her name which is rooted in Kybele, Ka'aba.

If we step away for a moment from the feminine genderisation of Cybele and into the alchemical feminine constructs of weight, measure and mass, we land firmly into the ground of near eastern properties of measurement, that of the Cubit and the Kabala. Etymologically linked with the Holy of Holies in Mecca, the eastern corner of the Kabba is facing towards the rising star Canopus (Alpha Carinae), there you will find it has the remaining cemented the fragments of "the black stone" a highly regarded artefact of the Islamic faith.

The root of all cabal and Cybele type phonetics are shared with words which mean crypt, cave, temple, skull, head and dome, which in many parables and texts are places where we can associate to the containment or place where a holy spirit can reside. However, in ancient ideology, the significance of the mother's womb is equivalent to the primordial waters of creation. The dark place where souls without bodies or form reside. The womb, therefore, takes on a much more existential significance in pagan religion. Plucking a child from the womb is equivalent to plucking a star from the heavens, or a soul from the abyss. The Mother-Goddess and indeed the sanctity of all motherdom represents a doorway to the physical realm from the celestial realms; and the worship in the temple womb merely a euphemism for the act of intercourse, which is probably the origin of the concept of staunchly patriarchal priesthood as they have maintained into the twentieth-century simply because it is only when the concept of sexual intercourse is aligned with "entering such a temple", that man plays his part in the creation of life, the

woman herself is the temple.

Here Cybele is depicted on her throne with two lions at each side the same as Rea.

Kybele - Magna Matter. Mater Kubileya (Mother, cube or measure of god) Kabalah!

O'sun (Yoruba Goddess)

The Blessed Mother of Nigeria, this river goddess associated to Venus is pronounced as the orthodox frame of academia will tell you "oshoon". Purposefully spelled in such way to imply an African tongue. But "oshoon" can be correctly pronounce 'Ocean' to our English tongues. Because O'sun, fertility goddess forms the life force of the waters in the river Osun which flows through Nigeria, southwest of Egypt in the continent of Africa. The river is is Nigeria's Equivalent of the Nile and even though three and a half thousand miles lie between them the essential spirit of the water goddess shares many parallels.

O'sun epitomises the channel like energy we receive from the Mother Goddess for what is humanity but the eternal continuum of the feminine *mata*. I saw just the other day a picture which really resonates with the idea of the eternal mother. As you may know, or maybe not, our mothers or ourselves if you're lucky enough to be female reproductive system contains the eggs of every potential child they are ever going to conceive right from birth, or rather slightly before birth. Which means that the material mother portion of your existence, was in your mother when she was still inside your grandmothers' tummy. Within the expectant mother exists not just her daughter, but her granddaughter or grandson. Three generations occupying the same physical space. An incarnate holy trinity. This infinite *mata* shows how the source of material in nature consistently ebbs anew for three generations but ceases with the male line. Firmly establishing the triune originating not from a masculine patriarchal hierarchy in antiquity but the mother feminine Goddess. Which forgotten occultism has been there before our eyes in such places as even the Tarot.

This Empress card from the 14th century Rider Waite deck clearly labels the Empress association with the number III and the river flowing to her left from its source.

The name O'sun is derived from the word *Orisun* which means 'source', and I have, over the years laboured the point of the Egyptian God *Horus* being the origin the word 'Horizon'. Here, I revise that claim, and now say that Horus of the trinity in the Egyptian pantheon is simply an equal half of two holy trinities. The Egyptian Pantheon of the patriarchal branch lead to what most of us now know as Christianity.

Osun is the equal Triune (Holiest of Trinities) on a feminine harmonic balance, there were two holy trinities. The Mother, Daughter and The Holy Ghost. The Holy Ghost so named as it represents the third of succession, which in the trinity can be either male or female, as the cycle must always end in a male.

The male represents the death of the cycle and it is referred to as the holy ghost as it exist unfertilised in a kind of quantum state, as Schrodinger's baby for want of a better explanation. It seems that if the 3rd generation foetus is male, the line ends with the death of the continuum, whereas if female, the cycle continues as the mother becomes grandmother, daughter mother and so on. Which ties in nicely with her myth story in which the *Ifa Literary Corpus in Ose Otura* says that O'sun was the only primordial spirit that was female amongst all the spirits that were sent to create The Earth. The male spirits ignored her and so she gathered together all female spirits.

Toil as they might the male spirits were incapable of creating The Earth and so they went to Olodumare (the supreme God of the Yoruba people) and asked why they could not create, in Oludumare's wisdom he told the foolish male spirits "Nothing can be created without Osun and her feminine counterparts or Syzygy[16], where she is named as their leader, they are called the 'Ajẹ'" and that anything man tried to do without women and without the forces of 'Ajẹ' was doomed to failure.

You may have noticed the word Orisun does somewhat constitute the Egyptian names phonetically which are Horus, Osiris and Set or Isis, and sun.

In Latin America, O'sun is called 'Mamae Oxúm' (pronounced Mama Yoshum') referring you back to chapter

---

[16] Syzygy – The first division or counterpart of a primordial source which is part of an equal and opposite pairing, the Aeons, archons or archetypes should also always have an opposing balancing force to their entire essence. Syzygetic, the conjunction of two cosmic bodies.

two, *The Bovine Goddess*. You can see the syncretism to all these belief systems and phonetics come into play across languages.

If we now take the Yoruba word for mother, it is "Iya Mi" or "Iyami" which means divine mother. It is taken in two parts from the word 'Àjẹ́' (the Aje as mentioned a moment ago) and Ami. Aje represents the essential spiritual self-infinite creative potential of the feminine aspects, particularly in their "birthing roles" and extends cosmologically into to the Odù, the source of the cosmos and creator of the universe *Orisha Odù* (the same as Orisun). I would like to claim that the *Ami* portion of that word represents the physical presence, or cumulative product of the spiritual force. As that links the one of the fundamental concepts of Gnostic Hermeticism, The *Iam* which I have covered and expanded upon in my other books. Particularly EgoSum which was almost dedicated to it entirely.

Meirothea

One goddess that really captures in name the truest name of the Goddess is barely known in common parlance, and that is Meirothea, Meiro means Mary, Mother, Omega and all the symbolic connotations across the spectrum of mother characters, if I had my way then as Yahweh is now commonly accepted as the name of the father god of the bible, then Meirothea would be the mother goddess. I do have very strong doubts as Yahweh being the name of the father spirit, as this Arabic demon entity of winds and sand where Yahweh originates is only one of the lesser demiurge in my opinion, and I have yet to discover a personal equivalent in the male equivalent that truly satisfies my understanding, Athor being currently the closest. There is I believe a resounding understanding within all women, that know they are already the Goddess incarnate, Men still have a way to go to realise that they too are the Goddess incarnate since we have allowed the divisions of hierarchical subtypes to make us identify with a specific label and make that label become who we are. But gentlemen readers, be not afraid to embrace the divine feminine self for self-imposed fear of what we would call in the seventies sissydom, a moral created by rules of society, the manliest of men are presented more by their physical appearance than their wits, and it is the goddess which is presented in our physical self. We are a spectrum of defining features, denial of self is deconstructive, we excel when we stop trying to make the world fit to an artificial self, the world will adapt to you if you tell it to. The first emanation prior to the division in which all things became. The Atma if you are versed in the works of the Theosophist such as Baily, Leadbetter and Blavatsky. Barbelo originates in the Nag Hamadi scriptures, and I do implore you to read such works as the Apocryphon of John, and particularly to "First Thought" which I would have loved to included in this book, however translations are subject to copyright and my translation would be a lot of work for something already more adequately done by others. It is freely available to read online however with a simple search. The text in line with Abrahamic scriptures till holds this hierarchy which places the father with higher precedence, however we know that this is driven by the politics of that century and this book hopefully will have corrected that order of precedence, to the true nature of the womb of the universe. If we consider Jesus to be the male aspect of God incarnate, then Meirothea is presented to us as both his mother and his consort, Mary of Madeline and Mary of Bethlehem, Of course Meirothea would also have a similar consort relationship with both her son, Jesus and the male god counterpart I refeed to for want of a better word as Athor, because Yahweh seriously doesn't cut it for me. Her consort is both earthly in Jesus and spiritual in the her male syzygetic counter essence.

What we have stumbled upon in the scriptures and a philosophical paradigm is the chicken and the egg argument of which came first. Which will always be a quandary if we insist on not dissolving ourselves of the hierarchical nature of order. We must accept that "in the beginning" the beginning came as a result of a division, where a distinction between now and then could only be measured by the division of now and then, before that there was neither state of "now and then" to compare. Each created the other which created "the beginning" as a third child of that order. This is the trinity of order creating itself.

The Pent Commandment.

The Bible has been adapted and translated many times throughout the centuries with significant changes to its text to suit the demographics of the region and times that adaptation took place. Within its cover many people have found that those adaptations suit their needs. But for the esoteric mind which is driven by the insatiable need to find one's own purpose, something within us seeks divinity at its source, in that we seem to hold more value and credence to the earliest versions of texts than we do in later interpretations. This may be primarily due to the sense of feeling we get, that if we are reading another's interpretation, we are influenced by that person and their personal subconscious bias. Their Bias like ours is influenced by the socio-economic and scholarly environment they have found themselves in, but most of them will have been oblivious to their predispositions and biases when they apply their interpretations. Many of the explanations of biblical texts I have placed in my books over the years will have a consistent underlying bias towards the principles I call hermetic knowledge. Your acceptance of these principles will only be adopted if they are an extension of your own current corpus of truth, or are not in direct conflict with your approved internal vision of the subjects. We cannot help it, prejudice based on experience is our nature and the way we construct all our personal views of "what is" historically, spiritually and scientifically.

Should I in some way produce sufficient extensions and comfortable explanations of these teachings, then you may well hold my writing in high regard; should I produce claims which take huge leaps from your current topic experience, then they will be seen as conjecture and laughable leaps of faith, making my writing contemptuous and discredited in your mind. This is the nature of our adaptation of knowledge, the author or tutor must build on experience to be understood clearly. In doing so, we are hard pressed to reverse deep rooted beliefs, but we can slowly chip away and the subject of theology and philosophy is divisive to say the least. Wherever you find yourself on the ladder of theology, we explorers of the "philosophy of why" will always find greater value in older texts, like they are in some way a kind of inversion to the progressive nature of observation we call science. We consider probably irrationally that the source of divinity must surely be found by looking back into time, to our ancestors, primarily based on our geographical or national identity, and then further afield into religious philosophies we find a connection to, but always we seek "the source" as opposed to looking to the future for greater understanding.

In the earlier chapter, *the synodic cycle* we spoke about the significance of Venus in her role as the feminine celestial character. In other books I have covered the twin natures of the character Mary, "the mother of God" according to Christian teachings, and Mary of Magdalene. I claimed they were representations of Venus as morning and evening star, present at the birth and death of Jesus the solar light. I believe, we need not see these opposing entities Mary the Virgin, Mary the whore as real people anymore, but as an allegory for the creative nature of the feminine mother goddess, who unlike the perpetually absent father character, she is wholly responsible as a virgin for the creation of the sacred child which is credited to be the light of the earth.

To draw in further bullet points that I wish to direct you to clues which lead to insightful conclusions, Venus is greatly aligned to the number five, a serpent shaped character when represented in its numeric form 5 is transposable almost with the serpentine the letter S. The aforementioned chapter included the diagram of the orbit of Venus and its connection to the symbol we call the pentagram, reinforcing the relationship, numerically the sister planet of earth is ordinal 2nd planet from the Sun , and so Earth being third we can simply add the two numbers for concordance to get their solar relationship has a value of five.

The word 'Pentagram' can be understood to mean five letters, as "Pent" we are understood to mean the number five. Pentagram, the five-pointed star that is so familiar with those with even the most basic of understanding of world of mystical knowledge, is 101 of occult study showing its divine precedence over all other occult symbology. But in the 14th century, almost a precursor to the publishing of the King James Version of The Bible, a new word is adopted into the English language, as if from nowhere "pent".

Pent, in its remnants of other modern usage denotes the build-up of force, or of an energy which has potential unrealised as yet, almost a direct definition of the potential for creativity, most often used to describe a rage or fire within one's soul, establishing phrases we have like "pent-up anger". But, in its earliest description the word *Pent,* seems to be akin to the word "occult" in that it means hidden, rarely will you find any reference to this historic meaning of the word "pent" but as scholars of the occult arts if we consider the nature of all forces that are hidden, they must always refer to a truth as one never hides a lie, what would be the point? No, hidden word is always the truth and so our mind tells us, that seekers of truth must lift the veil on the falsehoods which prevent our understanding of all things.

The mere fact we question who we are as a species, as life, as unbound consciousness, and the answers not being obvious to our understanding, we conclude that the truth must be contained within a secret, obfuscating veil of lies or half-truths. The land of beauty which lies beyond the seas is hidden by those very waters of deception, appearing transparent on close inspection, but greatly awash with its enormity and breadth of coverage that no one can see the land promised to the adventurous mind.

In that mariner-esq metaphor which almost reads like a treasure map of words, we find that when we look deeper into the significance of the origins, and the sources of our ancestors writings, we may find deeper meaning to the essence of the word more than its direct translation. Our volcabulary extends and evolves along side us, and words used in the past, were localised to regions and time, they covered a less fragmented understanding than we have now. This understanding is the mastery of awakening, being able to read occult texts is much like astrology and connecting the dots which form the pictures in ones mind, pictures for which words will fail. Indeed I would suggest that the secrets of the occult are much less hidden than hard to vocalise for it is a language of concepts. The great secrets are not always purposefully hidden, instead they are explained in many metaphors as they can be considered only visible in the minds eye. Like colours, no matter how you try, no matter how obvious they appear you cannot express them, you can only compare them to other things the student can compare to. Such is the nature of the occult.

The mother of manifestation, of our existence in the prime-material realms is almost mathematical in her design, we have five extremities of limbs, convenient for the mainstream esoteric writers if I dare include myself, which we are eager to point out to us on a very obvious level matches with symbols like the picture to the right.

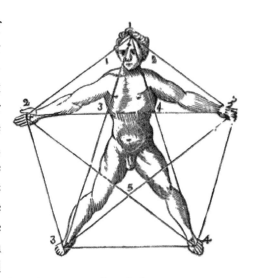

In such pictures, the human disappointingly never fits quite perfectly into this symbol; however, the representation does suit many an ideal. We have five fingers, five toes, we have five primary senses; sight, smell, sound, touch and taste, although there are many more. The four elements have also had their dominion extended to include spirit as an ethereal article added to the elements to fit into the body of all that the pentagram may represent according to Pythagorean teachings.

Indeed, great significance is applied to the number five in its alignment with humanity and our physical presence in the universe, and as I see it particularly favourable to the mother goddess.

As I recall in my upbringing in a [17] *CofE* school, in my Cheshire hometown of the United Kingdom. We were taught that the ten-commandments included two sets of five commandments. The first five sins are against God, the practice of faith and commitment to God, the second set were sins against our fellow man, beginning with "thou shalt not kill" as the sixth commandment. Other than the primordial order of sins and their severity, not much notice was paid to the significance of the numeric order. Thou shalt not kill, being seen as the most heinous act, and so highest-ranking sin against humanity finding place in the second half at commandment number six, closely followed by "thou shalt not commit adultery" which seems in the modern age not even worth of punishment by law, let alone a sin worth of eternal damnation.

But what I have found interesting in my later exploration in seeking purpose in existence by re-evaluating fables and mythology in ancient texts under my guise as an occultist, is that in the original [18]Septuagint, commandment number five was not seemingly a sin against God, but more towards our relationship with our fellow men, but specifically our immediate family, "Honour thy father and thy mother". Surely that should reside in the second half of the ten

---

[17] The Church of England, Protestant.

[18] The Septuagint (from the Latin: septuāgintā literally "seventy"; often abbreviated as 70 in Roman numerals, i.e., LXX; sometimes called the Greek Old Testament) is the earliest extant Koine Greek translation of the Hebrew scriptures.It is estimated that the first five books of the Hebrew Bible, known as the Torah or Pentateuch, were translated in the mid-3rd century BCE and the remaining texts were translated in the 2nd century BCE.

commandments along with other sins against your fellow humankind.

In later editions to fit the division of sins against gods and against man, some Bible revisions have switched this around to number six with the emergence of the Samaritan Pentateuch. The Samaritan Pentateuch, also known as the Samaritan Torah, which is a text of the first five books of the Hebrew Bible, written in the Samaritan alphabet and used as scripture by said people.

What has occurred to me, is that maybe the phrase "Honour thy father and thy mother" is not quite as physical as we would immediately believe. Maybe, this is indeed a somewhat hidden bible message instructing us to the very nature of ancient Goddess worship, one along with many other occult mysteries revealed when you seek higher levels of occult understanding, which you will do once you have broken the first mental seal of Solomon. The fabled seals of Solomon are in your mind, they are a layer of understanding which allow you to see your world differently, and so when unlocking the seal of mind, one is able to revisit the ancient scriptures and see whole new levels of occult interpretation written between the lines of quite mundane and nonsense fables. Indeed, almost every film you watch, every poem you read, every painting you see will almost certainly contain some for of nod towards some esoteric truth on breaking a couple of seals, such may be the case here and the significance of having this particular offbeat requirement in fifth place of the ten commandments, fifth, that's quite high for such a sentiment in the cannon of divine laws of god.

As the fifth commandment, five being the number of Venus, and it being the last of the first five sins against the Abrhamic all powerful God, I question if commandment number five itself is instructing us as to the presence of the Mother Goddess, Venus. Since the word "Penta-gram" translates to five-letters in its most commonly accepted etymological path but fits very nicely with the potential energies of "pent", gram we also associate with weight, or mass, these conjunctive leaps are once again to numerous to go dismissed without further investigation. Five is the centre of ordinal single numbers, the balance to all things 1 2 3 4 **5** 6 7 8 9.

Its shape is derived from the Sun , below the horizon.

Historically the Pentagram has not been as demonised or associated with witchcraft and occultism yet was adorned by the church itself to represent the five wounds of Christ, or the five visible planets to the naked eye for those that adopt the path of the Bible being a book of astrological metaphors. In Islam, this relationship between Venus and earth is simply the five pillars of Islam.

The word Venus itself has five letters, beginning with the Greek letter V (Hebrew Vav). The very shape of the letter is both representative of the single point of a star, the roman numeral for the number five, and the shape of the serpent fang.

It was only later, again around the fourteenth century and after the increased use by occultist, mathematicians and people who have since been coined "Black Magicians" such as [19]Giordano Bruno, who increasingly used the symbol to represent observations in nature, that was at the time of increasing  worry among the elite of the practice witchcraftery throughout Europe, that the symbol became heretical in the church.

In modern 20th Century interpretation there has developed a distinction between the upright and the down pointed pentagram which is suggested to indicate positive and negative connotations towards neo-paganism and white-magick and the more satanic downwards pointing pentagram which fits well with a Mendes like goat head in the middle. While this makes for great aesthetic design, in sorcery the orientation of the pentagram has no real consequence as it simply forms the relationship with the subconscious ethereal

---

[19] Giordano Bruno (/dʒɔːrˈdɑːnoʊ ˈbruːnoʊ/, Italian: [dʒorˈdaːno ˈbruːno]; Latin: Iordanus Brunus Nolanus; born Filippo Bruno, (1548 – 17 February 1600) was an Italian Dominican friar, philosopher, mathematician, poet, cosmological theorist, and Hermetic occultist.[3][4] He is known for his cosmological theories, which conceptually extended the then-novel Copernican model. He proposed that the stars were distant suns surrounded by their own planets, and he raised the possibility that these planets might foster life of their own, a philosophical position known as cosmic pluralism. He also insisted that the universe is infinite and could have no "center". (Wikipedia)

self, to the material world on observation. It is a key, or gateway which when observed represents the name of the mother goddess in physical form known as the Tetragrammaton.

While it is apparent that the Mother has been somewhat hidden by the bible and its patriarchal hierarchy for quite some time, there is clear evidence to suggest that scholars, for whatever reason continued to hide the presence and significance of the Mother in the bible. One would assume that the interpreters, authors, and scribes would simply erase any mention of her presence if they were the pro-masculine patriarchy and devotee's of "our heavenly father" we are lead to believe, instead it would seem, at risk of their very lives if they were be accused of Heresy, seem to have considered the knowledge too important to allow to disappear forever.

The Fifth commandment "Honour thy father" and most importantly "and thy mother" as the fifth commandment, in the "five books" or Pentateuch, seemingly therefore is positioned with significance. In the fist half of the ten commandments aligns it with the sins against god, not of man. It is the fifth commandment, from the five books.

Venus in our night sky as both morning and evening star, Mary as both virgin and whore, present respectively at the birth and death of Jesus. We begin to develop a sense of form which establishes the relationship of the "Mother" character, a dualistic presence which on a grander scale could be understood to be the presence of a greater being which is present before birth, and after death in the same way these allegories state.

One could almost imagine something like this in terms of ourselves, our life as we come from nowhere, we return to nowhere. The vast womb of existence in which we enter this world from our mother who represents the earth, mass and the physical, as we return to her in death, dust to dust.

She could almost be written OIO or IOI in that she seems to be at the beginning and the end of our individual experiences of life, the Alpha and the Omega. If we look at the Hebrew word for mother, we find similar character formations אמא

Comprised of the letters Aleph, Mem, Aleph, it is pronounced "Ima" (eema) and an anagram of "I Am" which you will know has great spiritual significance if you have read some of my earlier books such as *Luciferinaism:Ego Sum*. Similar inversions of the code which reverses the suffix of words van be found in the word "Venus" itself, again covered in other books. Ve-sun, where the suffix Sun, is reversed "nus" and pertaining to the "eVe" of the Sun , following our prefix-article-suffix model of the mother. Significantly, see how like the morning and evening star, which encompass the beginning and end of our days, like the mother encompasses the beginning and end of our lives, we find the very core of spiritual existence in the sentence "I Am" I, representing the male spiritual incorporeal self, and am, the material mother, physical self, whose holy union is a divine unity of the two opposing universal elements which is the sacred child, you. VaV the Hebrew letter V follows this Mother eVe and אמא formula of two identical entities surrounding the Aleph or alpha sun.

We find the word Pent early in the Bible, its not much of a leap to find that there is no mention of a snake in the garden of Eden, that popular imagery is derived from artists impressions of the Serpent rather than the words themselves, indeed there is no apple either, merely a "fruit", again popular artists imagery have created eVe, the mother of all humanity, accompanied by a snake and an apple, but it was the <u>serpent</u> that tempted eve, and it was to eat from

one of the two forbidden trees in Eden, that of knowledge. The Name Tetragrammaton is broken into five elements, normally written in the absent areas of space that surround the pentagram, TE V TRA V GRA V MA V TON, where each V in that sentence represents one of the convergences in the spikes of the out edge of that symbol, 72 degrees apart.

The Tetragrammaton is also known as the 72 names of God, supporting the astrological connection, since we know that there are seventy-two degrees between each of the points of the star (5x72=360). Each of the Names of god must therefore be split into one degree for each of the seventy-two degrees, and five times for each of the names. Te will have seventy-two values, Tra will have seventy-two, Gram etc. Those five aspects each will have a bearing to the manifestation of the day and mother Venus's position in relationship to the earth.

It is significant that the name has been placed into the absent space of the star, rather than each of the spikes, as the mother or womb is the absence of expression and potential for manifestation to grow within. In this guise, it's almost claiming that the absence is feminine, opposing almost all I have ever said about the feminine being physical and the male being spiritual. Indeed, the word "Absence" is rooted with the Hebrew prefix "ab" which means father, and sense does not need my explaining its ethereal nature rather than a physical one.

I can only conclude, an inversion yet again of principles which reflects the cyclic nature of things where up will eventually become down. Is it possible that at the apocalyptic transitions between Aeons all things are inversed to restore the universal harmonics? In the earliest gnostic understanding the mother was indeed potential without expression. The womb was the void, the unexpanded space which became filled by the seed of man, the stars, the planets, matter itself could easily be interpreted as a male intrusion into this virginal space, and expanse of eternal nothing.

Who knows what the new Aquarian Aeon will bring, we are at time of writing experiencing the forecasted flip of the magnetic poles, The magnetic poles simply must have bearing on our relationships with the solar system, our orbit, our very polarity is changing and this may well bring about a shift at the very least of our physical orientation, who knows, maybe this event will shift our equator placing Greenland on the new equator, closest to the Sun , and Africa becoming a polar region of Ice. While we have been through such apocalyptic global change before, have we interpreted this change from the ancient texts, flood myths etc, being the actions of god, whereas the acts of God are the acts of a universal nature we are now able to align to such events.

The "Te" (Greek) of Tetragrammaton is akin to the word "to" it conveys a meaning of a journey or path, a connection or link in which a spectrum of experiences link these things together. These can be considered the seventy-two expressions within the spectrum between the period between the five states of the pentagram. Te, can mean both, joining or the nature of the relationship.

The "Tra" (Aramaic) meaning "gate" or "door", Which I will also cover in the next chapter, but for now, we can understand it to mean something akin to the seal of which the pentagram stands. The doorway to the fruit of knowledge that was offered to eve is tempestuous. In that unveiling this knowledge is the very fruit offered itself, and that to understand the name of god, is to understand the word of god, as "the word" is made of symbols and letters, and that these made up of the astrological presence of the mother, can be read from the stars and their positions in relationship to Venus.

"Gram" is rooted and familiar to us in English, we use it to form the word "gramma" and "telegram" it relates directly to the written word historically, but colloquially "gram" as in "gran-ma" and "grammy" relates to our grand-mothers. This very modern word surely cannot be credibly linked to some hidden secret and ancient meaning, of course not, but can we also rule out that there is a hidden subliminal language which is outside of the laws of time, and that root information cannot be in some way instilled in the greater consciousness which operates at a level we are yet to achieve, and what we see when we connect the word "Grammy" with "gram" as the feminine, is something which supports a timeless truth, while we experience time traveling from what we call past, to our present, it is only because we are observers inside that law that we conclude that all things must originate before us, yet the future is a product of potential which is not bound by time, potential always has been. In other interpretations it certainly fits with the feminine "gram" being a metric of weight, gr-am. The prefix of Gra-vity.

Eve of The Witch

Returning to Eve, a goddess in her own right as "Mother of Humanity" according to the Old Testament. Her wicked ways brought "EVE"il into the world. Did you ever consider Eve a witch?

Popular amongst followers of the left hand path is the character Lilith, who in my opinion is another metaphoric Morning Star, Lucifer, refusing to lay beneath Adam, in the same way Lucifer refused to stand below God, it's the same allegory Explaining the passage of Venus as the morning star rising before the Sun . Lilith cast out of the Eden spends her eternity giving birth to endless demons, which is simply another allegory for the "light bearer" bearing each "new son", "new Sun", new day.

Eve her "Virgin Mary" counterpart to Lilith's "Mary Madeline" character are one in the same, present at the birth of the new son, present at the death of the new son. There is a "Mary" of dualistic aspects which follows the son of god, through-out his 33-year life. There is great significance to this number Thirty-three in astrological terms, firstly we can double it as the "divining" rooted with "division" of paths can be interpreted to the forking of options to a binary state, one state for Eve and another for Lilith, or the interchangeable Mary's if you like, (lets not forget 33 degrees of Masonry).

And 33x2 = 66, add the final 6 that all occultists are trying to find the meaning to "666" and you actually get 66+6=72, one for each of the internal angels of the 360/5 pentagram = 72, the number of demons in the goetica. These are Lilith's demon children and the numbers of the beast.

"Let him that has understanding count the number of the beast: for it is the number of a man; and his number is six hundred three score and six."

Of course, that's not the absolute definition of this number of man, as with all worthy esoteric understanding, it is merely one of the levels and one of the interpretations you have to add to your understanding. There is no absolute definitive interpretation.

Eve, we are told was tempted by the serpent in classic biblical stories. What can we possibly interpret from this? Well firstly, who was "the serpent?"

Classicism especially art will depict the Serpent as a snake and the fruit as an apple. But we know there was distinctly two trees in Eden that were off guard, the tree of life and the tree of knowledge. Knowledge in a biblical sense can be simply interpreted as sex, as to "know" someone biblically is a metaphor for sex. Nice and simple alternative interpretation using modern word usage, the snake that tempted her could add credence to this, especially when we go on to explain Adam and Eve's fall from grace like Lucifer's and Lilith's, is condemned and they are cast out of Heaven, Paradise, Eden... and so on.

We can find alternative understanding when we look at the Serpents roots, Serpend from Hebrew is "NacHaSh" Which translates as "The Shining One" and it should be obvious to you by now what I am going to suggest "the Shining One" is. Eve, Eve and Sun, Venus. She consulted the pentagram as a diviner because "Ha Nachash" actually has three definitions from Hebrew. One is "the shining one", the other is "diviner" and the last is "Serpent" but we have adopted a single narrative of this story in the English editions of the Bible. The version of the story that is the most popular will always control the collective viewpoint. Eve is the (EVEning) star, she is the pentagram, she is consulted, she is the witch and the diviner.

Practitioners of the arts with a darker disposition will always seemingly favour Lilith, because of her strong feminine nature for refusing to lay below man, but Eve, Eve was the first ever witch and she like lucifer refused the order of a god. The "Evening" when you consider it, is about the balances of nature, the darkness to the light. Lucifer or Lilith are not cohorts, they are both the morning star, bearing the children of the day, or bearing the light. Eve takes away the light, she is the true queen of the darkness.

Being cyclic, the eve, comes before the dawn, but then comes after the dawn and so on. It is these strings between the characters which bind them together that we must take from the ancient texts. The identities of the characters and their individual stories are for the beginners in the esoteric. For the advanced students it is the essence of their nature that must be absorbed into one's own understanding, this is the doorway to enlightenment. There are two 33 degrees of the earth in terms of Latitude and Longitude, and if you were to look at the convergence of the 33rd parallel of latitude that is 33 degrees north of the Earth's equatorial plane they fall directly on a mountain in the continent of North Africa called *Mount Hermon* just left of Damascus in the Lebanon. And to support a lot of the connections I am alluding to here, according to Pre-Bible stories of "the fall" of Man, of Lucifer of the Angels, of Eve, legend has it that this is the mountain where "The Watchers" or the Nephilim fell. The Nephilim were "the sons of god" who cavorted with the daughters of man in the book of Genesis. It's the same story again, and of course some will link this story to ancient aliens and genetic modifications, and I will neither endorse or reject that idea, the truth is I don't know, all I can really tell of is what I can conclude from the information I gather, I cannot rule it out, but I likewise cannot see any clear evidence. For me the fall of the Nephilim could just as easily have been a meteor shower such as the Taurids or a comet breaking up in the atmosphere and scattering across the sky would appear like the stars (angels) were falling from the heavens. I am however certain that the book of Genesis is purely a book of astrology.

Another story from the Old Testament is that of Uriah, and again we can link this story to our serpent allegory but first I must throw out to you some syncretic ideas from three pantheons of knowledge, Hebrew, Greek and Egyptian.

Left is a representation of an Egyptian Goddess called Wadjet as depicted on a carved wall in the Hatshepsut Temple at Luxor. The circle in the centre is the "sun disk" the head and tail arch over the disk depicting the womb or overarching order of the mother of the Sun such as Nun arches over the heavens as the higher order of motherhood. Looking back at the symbol, on the head side the serpent is rising, the tail drops below, these are the dualities of Venus in her relationship to the Sun and the story of the fall combined. Such simple symbolism operates on many-many levels. And if you turn snakes into staffs, another biblical metaphor we see the crook-staff of the shepherd used greatly in the Egyptian pantheon.

She is often depicted with two snake heads, again this is dualism symbology, and I draw your attention to the feet of the Gnostic symbol, Abraxas, remember that the feet are material and earth connective forces, feminine and grounded so the serpents are presented on this Gnostic Greek symbol as feet. The cockerel, who crows in the morning above the shield as both protector and the Sun - disk.

These three pantheons are all depicting the same concepts. Abrax and Therbeo were the names of the Horses (Horus) of the Sun according to Homer, referring you back to my cattle connection earlier in the book. Wadget was the nursemaid of Horus, tending to him and as a goddess she is protector of mothers. When Wadjet is presented with the Sun disk she is called Uraeus. Uraeus is from Egyptian mythology and is the serpent you will have seen on the forehead of the death mask of Tutankhamun, Uraeus is written in hieroglyphs as

Adorning the Uraeus is a symbol of Wisdom, like the goddess Sophia it is to be considered the crown or corona of the pharaohs symbolising their representation of the gods in human form with the wisdom of the divine mother and their rightful place as rule of the land, the material earth. By wearing the headdress over the pineal gland or the centre of the forehead also known as the third eye, they were charged with the duty of being the eyes of Hathor, a little known derivative of the Eye of Rah, or Horus.

Horus and Set both are depicted with this symbol, returning us to the morning start as Horus, and the Evening star of Set from which we get the words horizon, and sun-set.

The word Uraeus, is a compound of Ur which is the land of Ur, a "city" state in ancient Mesopotamia which represented all land, and another sharer of the root of our word "Earth" or "urth" and "eth" mentioned in the earlier Lilith section. Aeus, like Horus, Zues as a suffix, denotes area or dominion like radius phonetically from the "area of Ra" the circle or sun disk itself. Uraeus would be the dominion of earth or the entity charged with the kingdom of earth.

Folding back to the biblical analogies we can find the story of Uriah, which if you abstract the root information of the story you will get a very similar story to that of the birth of Christ.

Uriah was a soldier in King David's army, King David was an ancestor of the Virgin Mary in Christianity as she is described as David's lineage. The story of Uriah claims that while out defending his post for King David, David "knew" his wife Bathsheba who got pregnant from the encounter. Wanting to hide his misdemeanour David called Uriah from the front to return home quickly hoping he after his deployment would also sleep with Bathsheba as soldiers were ordered not to participate in sexual relations while on duty, this was to make Uriah assume he was the father of child. His urgent order to Uriah was to "come and wash his feet" which can be interpreted as absolving him of the responsibility of the earthly pleasure, cleaning away the feminine article. Uriah refused several pleas from David as he believed his duty was to remain with his fellow soldiers in battle. After Uriah repeatedly refused the orders David sent a letter to Uriah's commanding officer Joab to place him in the front line where he was certain to be killed. This parallels the story of Jesus, Mary in this case David then took Bathsheba as his wife, and their child died after 7 days, but a second child survived and despite not being the first-born son of David ascended to the throne and we know him as King Solomon. An important note to remember is that David was later berated for his transgressions by the prophet Nathan who told him of a parable of a rich man who had many sheep and a poor man from whom the rich man took the one ewe of the poor man to give to a traveller, I'll not detail this but the ewe is important later, or the sheep, or even the concept of shepherd-hood.

But the important context in which this story lies is the father of a king was not the husband of the mother of the child. Bathsheba, as a wife can be considered pure, whereas upon being seduced by David who also represents the harlot of Mary Magdalene. And like Eve, Bathsheba was also tempted by Satan into sleeping with David against her better judgement. This time Satan appeared in the form of a bird. Bathsheba was bathing behind a screen or obfuscated from view in a real context. David saw the bird and shot at it with his arrow, breaking the screen in two and revealing her unbridled beauty (Sanhedrin 107a) of the Midrash. In the biblical book of Chronicles, Bathsheba is spelled Bathshua, linking her to Jeshua another name for Jesus.

Now the "Daughter of Oath" is the literal translation of the word Bathsheba From Hebrew עֶבֶשׁ תַּב (bat shéva'), from תַּב (bát, "daughter") + עֶבֶשׁ (shéva, "oath") and this brings us full circle back to Mount Hermon, as Mount Hermon is "The Mountain of Oath" according to the Qasr Antar inscription. Qasr Anta is a sacred building at the summit of Mount Herman whose inscription was translated to read "According to the command of the greatest and Holy God, those who take an oath from here." And it is attributed to those fallen angels who undertook an oath together which was bound to a curse to "only take human wives" according to the book of Enoch and the name of that god was Ba'al, Ba'al-Hermon Lord of Hermon and the stone represents the palace of the lord. Since Bathsheba is the daughter of oath, then she is linked to Mount Herman, and indeed she has been taken as a wife by King David who we can now consider to be one of the Nephilim. Ba'Al translates to "God is coming" so when we apply that to the Mother of God, or the mother of Solomon where Solomon is Sol(sun) and Mon(moon) as extensions of the male female union. It completes the hidden meaning.

Ba'al finds his (or more likely her) name from the stories of the God Attar. Attar a semitic god you may be more familiar with her other names which include Ashtar, Athar and Ishtar or Inanna who has her own chapter in this book. Crossing genders according to culture Attar is portrayed as a "god of war" linked to, you guessed it Venus and was known to bring water to men, fertilising the land. Similar to the moon which we know affects tides, maybe even the star sign Aquarius (Aqua-ius, water dominion), the water bearer because in astrology and Greek Mythology this ties nicely with our story of David and Bethsheba, Aquarius is Ganymede, a Phrygian Nymph, considered male who was the son of Tros the king of Troy in who in turn was married to the daughter of the river goddess Simoeis. Similar to Bethseba Ganymede was spotted by the God Zeus while Ganymede was tending to his flock as a shepherd (I did say I would come back to the concept of shepherd-hood). Zeus who immediately flew down to him in the form of a bird, stealing him away for himself and taking him into the heavens where he continually serves as a water-bearer the form of "a bird", the links are undeniable in my opinion. The region of the skies where the constellation Aquarius resides is also "coincidentally" the source of a regular meteor shower, the largest of which is the Delta Aquarid meteor shower in late July and early August.

The Doorway, Knowledge.

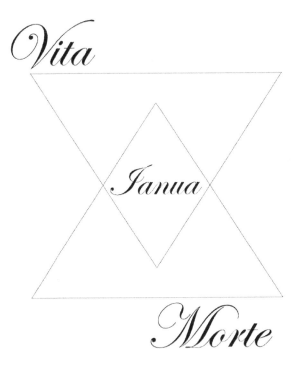

Between birth and death is the evolution of self and knowledge of all. The old are more accepting of death as during their passage of time we absorb universal truth. "The Door" between life and death is the ultimate knowledge of all things. Knowledge is attainment of death. In Hebrew it is the doorway, named Daat, where we root our word Death. In Latin the word "Ianua" or "Janua" where we root our word January, the beginning of the annual (Iannual) cycle, the death of the old year, and the beginning of the new on the 7thd day marked post the birth of the new sun on December 25th, December the 10th Embers or flames.

Knowledge of the esoteric can bring with it, knowledge rarely held by those in the span of their life. The symbol above, shows this process of life as we are born, purely vital and alive we rebirth with nothing, no knowledge at all. But potential, which is infinite, shown by the horizontal plane at the top of the upper triangle.

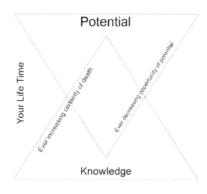

As time passes, your potential reduces to fixed outcomes, but with more knowledge. The certainty of your future becomes fermented in history.

Closer to the doorway of death, knowledge seeps through as you eventually begin to lose the material elements of your body. Age and decay takes it from you, and the sentience and acceptance of eternity becomes more of the essence of your soul. There is no doubt, we are reborn as all is cyclic after a period of returning to all knowledge, we are reborn with none.

January, Janus, JahNus, Venus. Is the rebirth into the physical realms from the spiritual realms? Etymologists will simplify the god of beginning Janus and being the fist month in our calendar as it fits their simplistic view of a very esoteric knowledge system, only cicero came close with identifying that Latin 'ire' meaning 'to go' presents foundation to this name. 'Ire' "to go", is paired with this two-face aspect of Venus, 'Via' to pass through, and 'veni' to come. The three aspects which compose the trinity of "Trivia", the three paths.

Janus is not simply 'to go' as claimed, but all three, the transition from old, to new and the transition between itself.

Jah(Yes) Nus (No) the polarities in absolute opposition creates the rebirth in the same way man and woman opposing elements create all new life. Janus is the god of doorways, gates and beginnings and the new year is a similar concept to our own cyclic existence in reincarnation. Venus and Janus, The doorway into life is via the Yes or No, VaJeNah.

Janus is an evolution of the Sumerian Goddess Inanna, circa 4,000$_{BCE}$, and as usual is simply defined by the regurgitating academics as "Goddess of love, beauty, sex, desire, fertility, war, combat, justice, and political power", is it getting a bit boring yet? She is also unsurprisingly associated with the planet Venus and has the full name of "Inanna Ishtar" where she was merged with another deity, Ishtar and Inanna of course we know are

one in the same, evening and morning star, you can consider Ishtar both 1stStar or morning star or equally phonetic, East-Star, also morning as the Sun rises in the east, Venus seemingly preceding it. We can conclude that Inanna is the evening aspect of that planet.

The Ve is a force which has presented itself as love, as life and as war, which is why the orthodox historians, but it is not in itself those things, but how Ve presents itself. Imagine Ve as "the attraction", the element of desire which is the initiate of motion. And so, this desire can be presented as love, but it can also be presented as envy, want and time. Its motion pulls the subject towards an inevitable rise and fall, which is a universal law. And so, the Ve presents itself in the form of a wave. This wave is universally present in all things, as all things are an emanation of a spectrum between two opposites.

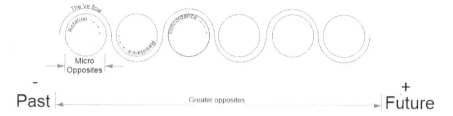

When you adopt this principle in all things it will give you the wisdom of the Sophia, Goddess of this particular aspect, whose Greek name is equivalent to the Roman Venus.

For example, if we look at a relationship, it begins with an upward flow of enthusiasm, in concordance with the rotation of the wheels of the wave. During its decent it becomes more and more influenced by the resistance forces of the next wheel it travels through, even though the wheel is rotating in the same direction, the wave passes underneath instead of over the wheel which creates resistance, this opposition to Sophia, could be presented as Apollo, a-polar inversion. Which reminds me of "apology". Let me tell you about the battle of apology. Often the breakdown of a relationship is caused by what I like to term the battle of apology. On the resistance downward transition of a relationship, you (I use you, but it can be any one of the couple) feels undervalued or offended in some way, even very slightly. The emotional oil to ease this resistance comes in the form of an apology, sought from the other person. The affirmation that the other person has realised their mistake, or wrongdoing releases endorphins which are addictive, highly addictive. The emotional gratification once sought in the affirmation of desire on the positive upward path once you reach a relationship zenith can only be matched by the negative downward oils of resistance. Upon receiving apologies from your partner, you seek more apologies instead of positive unification, you begin the process of opposing resistance, and so your mind subconsciously seeks more and more faults with your partner, to which you can hope to obtain the oils of apology. It gets to a point that no matter how hard your partner tries at this stage; you will always find faults with them. Meanwhile you're desire for more apologies grows in momentum. To the point where despite feeling that you love someone, you still dislike them, and everything they do and you end the relationship or they do, being fed up of your consistent criticism.

However, if you are aware of this and you want to change the situation then you simply must find new zeniths for your relationship and dismiss any criticism you find yourself making. Most people, not being aware of this universal mechanism will find that their lives and relationships are a series of ups and downs, as eventually, even being unaware of the universal principle of waves, you will ride that wave through the lower half, and begin on the upward path again, for a while.

This is an example of the wave form in relationships, but it applies to all things, another example will be work, you get a new job, you ride that wave of love, as time progresses you will find more and more faults to the point where you hate it, and this addiction to negativity to oil the resistance replaces where once the friction of positive carried us. When we are moving in the same direction, we need that security friction, to adhere us in the same direction, we work with it. However, on the downward slope we resist the friction and desire the oil of freedom. Opposites within opposites, wherever we are it is the subjective opposite forces that we utilise.

In ancient mythology Venus was the apis-heffer which pulled the Sun across the sky, it was that very force, in northern mythologies we had horses, other cultures used bovine animals, which were more suited to the motherly, milk providing metaphor.

The Gender Kingdom

Since the physical body has the feminine gender, and the spirit has a male, these universal archetypes conflict within us and we become the catalyst of transition between the two dynamics. The body, which is under the domain of the ego, recognises its own failings, and seeks a spiritual harmony with its opposing male counterpart which criticises its failings, the spiritual self is of course considered an idealism in its purity and can be nurtured within the mother to higher values, yet it is the same higher values which present themselves as our unachievable morals. This dynamic becomes the essence of a cycle within oneself to strive for progression, improvement or ascension in the upwards cycle, but also the criticism, self-doubt and flaws we see as laws preventing such ascension. When we realise that both are products of the psyche, then we can learn to manipulate them to our own advantage.

Ascension seeks a oneness of purity and the idealism of the kingdom. The Kingdom is the unity of the self. This is aligned with a spectrum of the body placing the head as high in the order where spirit resides and the feet, being furthest away from that pinnacle of physical representation of the spiritual essence within oneself. It could also be depicted as the serpent's tail opposing it's head. Feet are symbolic of Earth and our connection to it so they play an important role within classic interpretations of the Bible stories and later in the spiritually centred art movement.

Between the feet and your head, there are considered to be twelve points of transition between your physical manifestation and your spiritual manifestation. The body is a diagram of this transition which only represents the spiritual side, they are not as suggested in the yogic structure directly paralleled, so focusing on your feet in the way you would concentrate on the root chakra in yogic meditation would not provide any benefits, but symbolically in metaphoric literature and art, hidden understanding of symbolism can be found by being aware of these parallels, but that said, they do have relationships with their neighbouring spectral presentations.

1. Is the ground, or external matter, mother earth and all material components of the universe. You may consider this external to you, but it is not, the harmonisation of nature is to align the physical universe with the spiritual one. The unique you extends to all the universe as that universe extends to you.
2. The feet, symbolic connections with the ground and ego, they are what touches you to the earth, like the root of your life tree.
3. The heel, healing, your weakness and your countenance. In tales such as that of Achilles and his heel, is the ultimate artistic impression of that mystical science, consider heels to be your sapling spiritual growth, newborn and close to the Earth mother, but neglecting them is neglecting the structural foundation of self. They are youth and undefined potential.
4. The knee, part of the chemical marriage begins at this point and the merger to the more magickal you.

Magick begins at this point as the marriage of the physical to the spiritual begins to merge, form is taking place, the mapping of self, the architecture if you like.

5. Venus, the creative where the spirit becomes, physical. The midpoint and balance, where sex and gender are determined, masculine and feminine and all its spectrum between.

6. Organus, The creative centre of the new universe, the womb. At a higher level than Venus, this ascended self is not only your truer established self, but has the potential to create the eternal you through reproduction. This is the adolescent self which remains within you always.

7. The Sun, the light as versioned by the material. The solar plexus, a convergence of the external spirit father who sits opposite his consort Venus to create spirit within matter, life.

8. The love, The heart, passion and desire of the spirit towards the physical while heavily still within the realms of the spirit. The arcadian rhythms in which we can measure our frequency.

9. Throat, the word, counterpart to the knee within the architecture is the law, the will and the word, as commandment to the universal self.

10. Spiritual you, the spiritual ego, counterpart to the physical ego of the feet within you is the spiritual ego of the mind, whereas the feet are a presentation of material aspects, the spiritual you is more fluid, less rigid and can be modified to suit a presentation personality.

11. The crown, the kingdom, the governance of the whole, this is where your kingdom ends, in the way your feet end your physical, the kingdom ends your spiritual, but like the feet having a relationship with the eternal physical universe, your neighbour the heavens is the spiritual, nonphysical kingdom of spirit. Remembering we are the spectrum between the two realms.

12. The heavens, external consciousness.

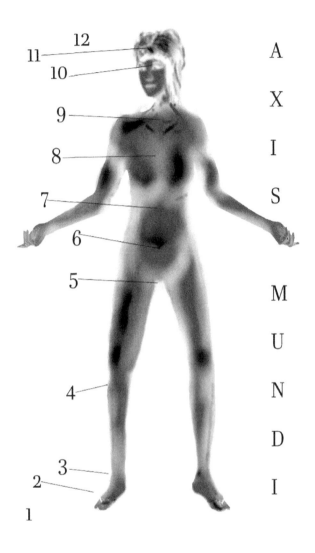

Notes on Woman a word.

Understand that we have been subject to much misinformation but revealed in the language is truths which are undeniable.

Take for example the word Human, modern liberalism has taken offence to the word Human as they believe it emphasises the male element of humanity by the inclusion of the word man, but this could not be more wrong. The word Human is a derivative of the word "woman" think "whoman". The nature of the life of a person is that of a woman, the physical expression of all of us is *whoman*. It is a reference to the body in which the seed of life is placed, Woman the creator, woman without which there is no life in this universe. Man in the word Human is merely an appendix to the whole state, woman is inclusive of the whole representation of human, they're pretty much the same word before gaining distinction by spelling in written form, dialectal transference by phonetic interchange in the period which amalgamated the root structures of words we now know as English.

To the extent female, male is rooted with "mal", it is a negative appendage to the pure "who". Female begins with the iron element FE, ferrous, Ferrier, bearer and carrier of spirit within the iron mother, matter. the marriage extends this as the Hus band, is the male who is bound to the female 'who-bound', and house, hus. Which refers to the astrological passage of Horus, where the son resides in the house, of astrology. Akin to a child being born into the house of the who-taurus, *Taur* being the eon of the Taurus, and the travelling through the star signs where we find the root word "tour".

The Annul Ven

It is essential to understand the influence Venus has on us astrologically as an archangel it is one of the nine angels (angles) that is responsible for manifestations and actions in our prime material plane here on Mother Earth. She has unbound power at the correct time of the year.

Speaking of times of the year let me introduce you to utilising Venus's sphere of influence. Being a goddess with dominion over the physical, she in her aspect as Lucifer, the morning star. I'm sure you're very familiar with astrology to some extent, even if it is only for reading your Horoscope. Well, the reason you have something called a horoscope is related to Venus, and, as I mentioned earlier, Venus's relationship to Horus. Your Horoscope is your Horus-scape or Vescape. The letter V is incredibly important. It simply represents an angle of exactly 72 degrees from the centre to each of the five points of the pentagram. And if we reduce the number 72 (7 and 2) then add them together, we get the number nine.

Seventy-two is a very interesting number I have written about several times. But it does have other exceptional properties. If you take two from seven, you get five, the number of points in a pentagram. Maybe that doesn't seem that intriguing to you but let us just see some more. Weirdly all the angles in a pentagram, seem to reduce to 9

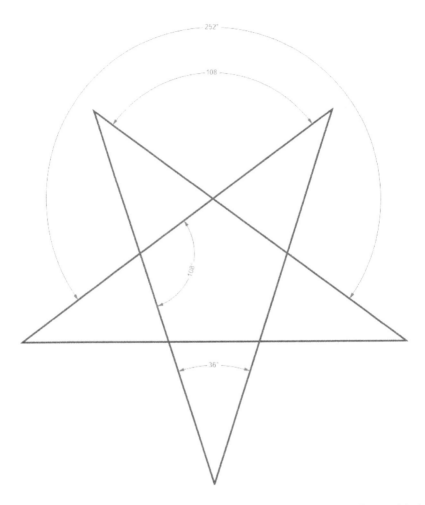

Because we get this recurring combination of angles which include the numbers 1and 8, 2 and 7, 3 and 6, 4 and 5 and occasionally with a zero, or O as it represents the whole.

So the whole 360 is 3+6+0 and since the whole can be reduced to 9, all its equal components also must reduce to 9

So if you divide 360 into any whole number, such as 12, one for each segment of the Horus-scape we get 30 as 360 will divide into 30 segments of 12 or 12 segments of 30.

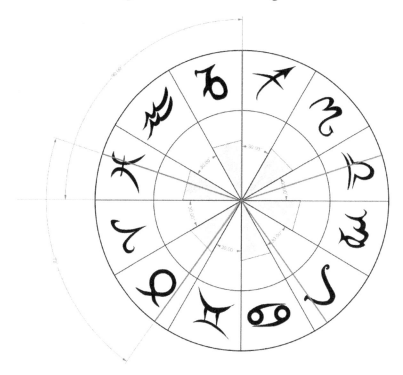

In Red the V, which is the arch angel (angle), V represents Venus. The 5 points of Venus or the pentagram. Rotates throughout the year.

It is important to note that 360` = 5 x 72` one for each point of Venus, and each degree of the 72` that makeup one of the 5

The 5 points represent the influence of Venus in her sphere, on the rotation of the wheel. Head being upmost, at all times, and his enlightenment represents the aeon where her head resides alongside the risen sun. The four remaining represents her Right and Left Hands. Used both as Morning Star Lucifer, towards Enlightenment, and the Sinister Left hand of Set, The Evening Star. Each has different attributes in the morning or evening, depending on the use of the right- or left-hand sphere.

This is our current astrological stance as we move into Aquarius with the five ruling arch angels, Aquarius – Head, Taurus – Right-Hand, Scorpio- Left Hand, Cancer – Right-Foot, Libra – Left-Foot.

The Horus or Hours of the clock should be read clockwise. And so in the above example, her left hand would be the first encounter from the head, this would be sunrise, left hand, which has dominion over Scorpio, and in the evening Libra. Signifying a time to strike, then a time to balance or to set laws.
Her right-hand rising is in cancer and her right-hand falling (even though it seems higher) is in Torus. This above image represents an ongoing astrological age as our head is just entering the epoch of Aquarius, but by aligning the pentagram to the actual calendar month on the head, we can get an immediate point of power where Venus will have her most influential actions as the wheel (whole) of the year is made up of the 360 days (or deities) that belong to the soul, or sol, or for some "god" as most religions are based on solar worship. And these are the 360` of the cycle.

And the remaining five days, belong to Venus, or Horus, the Egyptian Son of the God O'siris.

So as it happens today it is the 22nd July 2019 and so I place Venus head at the current date, in the sign of cancer to get an annual projection of today's spherical influences.

Here I show specifically the Head of the goddess in the sign of cancer for today.

This places Lucifer, our Rising star into Taurus, falling star into Pisces. The left-Hand path is our adversarial elements where we oppose authoritative constructs. Taurus the bull is a horned, and stubborn beast and Pisces, a duplicitous slimy fish. These I should apply to physical and material meditations, beings strong headed in the morning. And Duplicitous in the evening. For my spiritual side, today I should be preparing to act, the sting in my scorpion tale should be used early, don't hold my cards close to my chest. So that come the evening I can restore a balance, or a law.

These are the angles of 9

You see, each of the 12 astrological segments is 30`
(30`x12=360)
3+6+0=9
Each quadrant (astrological season) is made up of 3x30` (90')
9+0=9

There are four quadrants, of 90` totalling the 360`.

The pentagram, man will occupy 5 of the 12 segments. Leaving 7.

5x12=60

7x12=82

60+82=144 (1+4+4=9) (144/2=72)

The quadrants represent ages of the celestial year, Spring, Summer, Autumn, Winter. Each quadrant has 3x30` (90' sections) a "right" angle. The 72` of the pentagonal arch, plus the 90` of the seasonal arch = 162` 1+6+2=9

There are 360' which are in command of the soul, sol. These are the Days or deities. The remaining five are in the hands of man for each point of the pentagram. Align the date to the astrological pentagram, and you will know when best for your actions.

The Solstice Ritual

For the seasoned occultist, witch or pagan much emphasis is placed upon the biannual Solstice events as a period of celestial harmony. You may be well-versed to know that solstice originates from a term loosely meaning "Sun stands still", and it occurs at the times of the polarised winter and summer seasons at juxtapositions to the Spring and Autumn Equinoxes. These four events complement our four seasons, where the Solstices present the extreme conditions of a very long day (summer solstice), or a very long night (winter solstice) as these opposites.

The Equinoxes represent the absolute median between these extremes where the day and night are equal in their duration. What is often overlooked by the glorification of these events in the occultist calendar is the opportunity to find harmony in oneself instead of the alluring cosmic harmony, which is of course, observably greater than the self. Yet, we are a part of the whole; we are in our feminine aspect physical aspects which complement the celestial alignments as objective viewers experiencing this moment in time.

Woodruff Sheppard M.D., a supporter of Annie Besant's theosophical works inspired me to write this with an unrelated quip in his publication *An Outline for Beginners in Occultism* 1919 which reads:

Know: That that silence is a prerequisite to real
thinking, only through a mind stilled can come the
truths from higher sources.

I'm a syncretic follower of all belief systems, so you may find as I, his book or aged pamphlet to be more precise, a bit too Theosophical-Christian based for your particular taste. Although, when describing the study in a primarily Christian framework, he does suggest that other patrons may be applied to the principle. I suspect that at the time of writing, which was 1919 it was less scandalous to frame occult workings in such ways. That said, I did stumble upon the book for free, and I wouldn't suggest you go to any great lengths to source it. I mention it only in passing.

What impacted me most about this statement reminded me of the correlation between the soul and its insubstantial aspect, the mind and Sol, our sun. Using the preposition of [20]AASB, there are clear reflections in the celestial events and our personal sense of understanding that we really benefit spiritually in the absence of external forces and influences such as family, people, our work, our lives and general community interaction than we do simply being adherent to these influences. All seem to construct a representation of self to which we are mostly ill-fitted when we focus on that special essence which is 'the self'. The influences listed above often create a self-less hologram in which we shape ourselves to comply with the expectations of our social environment. Woordruff inspires me ironically to seek outwardly the spiritual self I find within, rather than allowing external forces to shape the spiritual self.

---

[20] As above, so is below.

This moment of stillness of the mind during the meditation on the solstice doubly enforces the stillness of the celestial soul, and the personal soul so that it becomes important to find who we are as individuals within the correspondence of the "greater you" extended to the celestial environment — ideally midday on any given solstice would be the ideal time to find the harmonics of self, soul and Sol.

The distinction between the two, winter or summer would be to determine what aspect of the self you are seeking to explore. The long night of the winter solstice is conducive to the feminine earth/water element, and the long day is conducive to the male air/fire elements.

What I would advise for those seeking to find harmony in yourself, is to identify those elements which you feel need further development. Often when getting guidance on meditation, we do so to focus on a particular concern, and in doing so, we bring from the *priMary* plane as binding chord which disrupts the mediation. This chord like the umbilical cord ties us to the womb of physicality; what we are trying to achieve is the unbound self- potential which at the end we can bring back into the primary plane. By taking our concerns with us to meditate upon, we are actually taking the concern with us into the self, making it much more a part of our reality. This is counterproductive. In meditation all connection to the physical realm should be abandoned, issues will be addressed by their order-natural and the meditation of self will reveal your true instinctual essences in the order that they need to be revealed. You are always where you need to be, and there are no shortcuts to personal development, that which is an obstacle for you is a lesson that needs to be exercised.

The purpose of the Solstice ritual is to find this essence of the potential you, the clean spirit which existed at your birth, without the corruption of your environment. The architect of self, much like if you were following the plans of building a cupboard from a flatpack furniture store, the instructions you read, need referring too every now and again to ensure you are looking at your personal greater design and not that shaped by your surroundings.

In her presence as prima-materia, mother earth is still a child of mixed gender, she contains us as children, as life, and she herself is imbued with life and so she is slightly lower on the architectural hierarchy than some other more "prima" material celestial objects such as The Moon, who's word begins compliantly with 'MO' like "mother". Lifeless, she holds immortal beauty of that which is absent of life. Mona (mono, one) is simply one aspect of the soul-atary sol (son) which combine to make life as the exotic material. the Sun should be considered pure life without matter, it is a heliotic substance. Whether the ancients considered the mass of the Sun as playing a part in their narrative is hard to tell, because of the subjective nature of our solar system, we orbit this object, and so all our measurement are relative to that local universal constant.

The Moon and her cycles have so much more influence on this planet than it seems Venus ever could have. Incidentally as we map our solar system away from its soul, providing it with the physical components which make up is body, Mercury followed by Venus have no moons, then The Earth begins this creative complexity by having its own satellite, Mona, Mona is a contraction of the name Madonna, and I may bring you in mind of the Di Vinci painting "The Mona Lisa" which can be read as "The Mother Isis".

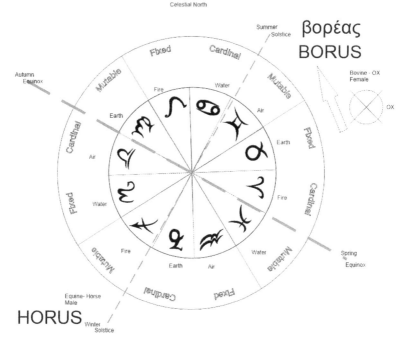

Above the celestial interpretation of the self-devouring snake Ouroboros which shows the cyclic nature of the passage of the year including the equinoxes from which ouroboros gets its name. Horus-Borus. Equine (horse) and Bovine (oxen) which make up the word Equine-ox.

Each of the four primal alchemical elements Fire, Earth, Water, Air have corresponding cycle phases of Mutable, Cardinal and Fixed, these expressions phase.

Mutable and Fixed phase in and out of the cardinal signs, replicating the waveform. Beginning with Mutable.

Mutable Pisces, Gemini, Sagittarius and Virgo signs are adaptable, fluid and open to exploration of possibilities. They are similar to the potential state in Gnostic creativity. Here comes into play the designer element where all options are open towards the goal of creativity. They are able to compromise or fit in and support the failings where the fixed and Cardinal signs have been locked in by their own Rigidity, mutable while having this somewhat negative connotation of "being silenced" does not necessarily infer any weakness, instead the mutable aspect is really the head and wisdom of the individual, while mutable, what the head and wisdom is doing is not silencing its own voice, but discarding (muting) the fruitless by applying wisdom, leaving only the orders which are to follow. Mutable signs represent inspiration and each of the elements is represented by a mutable element.

Pisces (Water), Gemini (Air), Virgo (Earth), Sagittarius (Fire).
when used in conjunction with masculine and feminine elements of The Moon and Sun we can build stronger male or female attributes in terms of physical (female) or spiritual (male) results. The omegic feminine mother signs favour is placed to likewise feminine and physical endeavours during this period. Contemplation of working with The Moon and The Earth in these months will be more fruitful. This is not to be confused with ruling planets, for example Cancer is ruled

by The Moon, but this does not make Cancer physical attribute, more that the physical moons planning stage in the Mutable Gemini period will have more "ruling" on the cardinal cancer, and therefore more likely the desired fixed result when we arrive in the fixed Taurus, law, result.

Consider them to be stages of projects, where Mutable is planning, Cardinal is doing, Fixed is results.

Cardinal signs express themselves in the celestial calendar at the beginning of the transitions. Immediately following the Equinoxes and Solstices, the mutable adaptation and planning has already resolved a direction towards the cardinal expression. The cardinals should be seen as "the plan" or "the principle" once all the options have been explored in the mutable aspect. These are the idealistic signs, the conclusions of planning, while not yet fixed we have a plan which we believe to be the ultimate solution. These are activity signs, they are the "getting it done" or doers, these are ideal times to put your plans into action, to take on the tasks that you have been planning to do. This manual labour is hermaphrodiac, the labour which presents the birth is as intensive as the labour that ploughs the field.

Aries (Fire), Cancer (Water), Libra (Air), Capricorn (Earth)

Fixed Signs are exactly that, set in stone, unwavering, strong and dependable.

The Offering, Sacrifice.

As rituals go within the realms of the religious, the irreligious and dark arts, there is none more troublesome than that of the sacrificial offering. The offering has presented itself in many languages and cultures in every corner of the world, no country or faith of history is without its presence in their darkest of guilts.

In the pre-Roman cultures of the Brittan's the word "Opfer" now translates to "victim" as a Proto-Germanic word, which is probably the way we now perceive a sacrificial subject. The word "victim" would suggest in its modern understanding, that the subject of the sacrifice would have had their life force removed from them involuntarily. However, in the case of sacrificial acts, most cultures which enacted human sacrifice to the gods or a greater than oneself concept, a sacrifice was very much a personal act of choice, the definition of sacrifice is considered self-loss but really means something quite different from the Latin: Sacer or Sacre, meaning *holy* it shares its root with the word sacred, and 'Facere' which means *to cause, enact* or *make effective* sharing its root with the word "fact" the feminine measurable aspect, the personal act of sacrifice, really means to "make sacred" and to "fix wholeness" but, by extension you cannot sacrifice something that is not yours to *sacrifice.* The only question of this loss is the concept of ownership of that which is lost.

One can sacrifice themselves, however in a very "legal technical clause" used as law often is corrupted to the benefit of those creating the law, one could argue the legal definition of ownership, to wriggle out of making the "self-sacrifice" in order to achieve self-gratification rather than the intended act of grand altruism.

Traditionally, in all cultures there shouldn't have been a case of people "being sacrificed". Instead, they were themselves sacrificing, a very noble, honoured and exemplified state of assertion to a holier state as an ophering to the gods, to become a part of that greater essence of the god. Their feminine physicality would be returned to the lifeless mother and their spirit ophered to the patron deity they were being sacrificed to.

So, we get this conflict between offering, in its modern tense "to give" and "to be offered" a different thing entirely. When we give something, we part with it, and remain intact, but less than whole, and sacrifice where we "make holy (whole)" is defined more as an act of self-restoration. The act of sacrifice describes a transition from one "whole" to another. In terms of the Black Arts therefore the word usage "Sacrifice" is contrary to their ritualistic intend, one could not sacrifice anything to the devil, as to sacrifice by definition is to "make holy", which I think is the last thing a black-magician wishes to do. Likewise, traditionally a sacrifice must be a loss from one-self. You cannot sacrifice another. However, all that being said, what we now call ritual sacrifice, including human did occur in many traditions, as much including Christian as any other Pagan, if not more-so, so no culture can take the higher moral ground here.

The Opfer (noun), where we get the English word "offer" also has a Hebrew phonetic sibling of "Opher", which softens the first syllable to the more familiar offer we hear today, in Hebrew the word means "fawn or stag", which is not a animal native to the Middle East and the orthodox roots of what we believe to be the Israel tribes. So, we can be confident that the word travelled south from the Northern Europeans regions. However, in the Middle Eastern regions the animal most similar to the Stag would probably be the goat, and that would suggest that animal sacrifices adopted in those regions to mimic the northern ceremonies would probably fall to the goat, or sacrificial lamb.

To understand the nature of the Opfering, we return to the divine separation of spirit and matter as defined by gnostic tradition. Spirit, male must be separated from material female. Returning the impure to the pure. Spirit alone in pure, matter alone is pure, they are virginal. Yet when they unite each equally corrupts the other. Life itself is the original sin, whatever form it takes, whatever side you take, spiritual or material while in our living form is sinful, because you are a corruption of the natural universal forces of the mother and the father characters.

Sacrifice itself can be made to honour either aspect of the divinities. Of course, the paternal "ab" (Hebrew for father) which forms the Ab-rahamic traditions will claim their paternal god to be the true god, maternal Goddess, "Mat" or "Gaia" the physical earthen Goddess believers will claim theirs to be the true Goddess. Whichever to which the opfering is made, makes one "wholly" of that order, you either sacrifice your body or your soul for eternity vowing never to return to the sinful world of corrupt "life". The belief either way declares that upon separation, the body, physical descends into the underworld and the spirit ascends into the heavens.

The Mother, being quantifiable as explained at the beginning of this book, is the true goddess of The Earth, Ea (derived for Gaia.

Now Ea, despite what you may have been told originated from the female earth and water goddess we know as Gaia (g-ee-eh (gea)).

History has since aligned 'Ea' with the Sumerian Enki as earth god who is overtly masculine, in line with the Abrahamic intent to obfuscate the true harmonic equality of the feminine goddess, and in doing so has managed to erroneously / intentionally switch the gender of Gaia to Ea, some of which because they again have mistakenly concluded that the hub of civilisation and the majority of our religious and spiritual beliefs began in Mesopotamia some twelve thousand years ago, but I, after many years of study into a more eclectic and syncretic investigation into to source of our beliefs have concluded that while the Middle-East is certainly been the most beneficial hub of ancient knowledge, was not the source, it merely is the host of worldly knowledge since it has been responsible for the earliest of known and translatable human writing.

We must remember that writing came much later to the collective knowledge of mankind and that writing is not the source of knowledge therein, it is merely the channel from which we perceive it. But what they wrote of, would include the tradition historical as they perceived them from the most common and established civilisation include those of the north, Mother godlessness's, and feminine bounty was celebrated long before this written documentation. The relief of the Venus of Laussel, in northern France depicts a "bountiful" mother goddess which has been dated to being over twenty-five-thousand years old.

The knowledge contained on those ancient cuneiform tablets most likely was an amalgamation and current context of gods from all of the known world, its traditions and beliefs which were much travelled, in the same way that most of Americas god, the Abrahamic tradition, Christianity etc, they were not American Gods. Yet, the traditions, customs and beliefs travelled as people traversed the globe. All we can truly conclude from the actual evidence of the cuneiform texts and its origination in the Mesopotamian regions, are that they were probably written down there because these people it seems invented writing. We cannot possibly conclude that the oral beliefs originated there purely based on the geographical location of the written texts. That would be like concluding that chickens are born in supermarkets simply because that's where we first encountered them (assuming you weren't brought up on a chicken farm). What we must do, as I have been doing is trace the linguistic patterns in their phonetics rather than written conjecture of translation. An example of such is above where "stag" is rooted in Hebrew, yet stags are not native to that region. Seemingly the evidence points for me to a more Hyperborean origin of many of the religious pagan concepts, which I believe travelled the world on the crust of the last ice age as the Hyperborean people were able to move south to more temperate climates making use of the land masses formed by ice which connected eastern and western continents. Interestingly supporting this linguistic crossover of the Celtic and northern tribes to the Middle East is that the word stag in celtic is "Damh" phonetically linking 'Damnation', and the word con-demn-ation". We see a historical link between these acts of sacrifice linking regularly terms across great distances and cultures between the Germanic and Hebraic languages.

The notion of sacrifice, even self-given has also been corrupted in the modern age we live in where people have used their deaths to murder others, nothing is more damning and contrary to the holy ordinance of sacrifice than that of what in reality is "suicide murder", I'm specifically referring to suicide-bombers and the likes but extending to people who believe they engage in "Holy-wars". The honour and purity of the opfering is sullied by any death which is not self-given, that includes traditional animal sacrifices. There are only two forces in play here, the male and female aspects of spirit and matter, mother and father, deaths in the name of either which was not wilfully given by the true owner of the life work as a negative force dishonouring the god which they have been ascribed to. So, for the suicide bomber who takes ten lives, he gives ten lives to the opposing factor, for his one.

The ultimate Celtic sacrifice was performed under what was called threefold law. To achieve blessing for the town a male of twenty-one years of age (three times seven) would be one of a few volunteers for union, or wholeness. Upon honoured selection he would spend a full year being blessed by the town's folk, who believed that the person becoming sacredly, whole again would be able to return blessings from the other side, spiritual. He would also have a choice of priestess who would join him on his journey, she too was chosen by him from a selection of willing participants. Together they would live like royalty until the time known as Imbolc and the day of the conclusion of the sacrifice. The Mother goddess granting her blessing for the crops, would favour one of the couples and bless them with a child in womb during the Imbolc period. The chosen coupling would on the sacrificial night embrace. Wooden steaks would be driven through their shoulders binding them together for eternity, with the unborn child in situe.

The Conclusion

Gravity is objectively identified with its source element matter, our mother, they are an expression of one in the same, gravity is the resistance caused when tears in the universe occur due to its expansion a void. This creates observable energy we call stars. This energy when spent creates matter to fill the missing gap in the created tear of the void.

This is the Mother goddess force which exist in the womb of eternity. An unknown goddess in which we are expanding. You could call it her womb. We exist id a dichotomy of thought and shape, and not just us as humans but as life itself in all forms, as the children of the great mother, the O-Mega , we are but expressions of her "in her image" so to speak.

The creation of matter is as mother, the negative attractive force which is such that an implosion could not be in a singularity. And so the singularity must therefore expand into the negative pre-universe. The mother sacrifices her perfection in a breach of her divinity, this sacrifice causes space to tear into her very womb creating existence, the residual energies pouring through that matter is alchemical father fire, drawn in to the material universe and creating all we perceive, now we can perceive without into our great mother.

The knowledge she provides is delivered through the inner id, the voice of the goddess, intuition, pre-knowledge, pre-mention. Knowledge of all ages, which exist within us as it exists without, the self that we ask for advice from our subjective ego self, she provides the divine purest inspiration.

and she too is aging and evolving with us, the universe is experiencing a unified growth, even with civilisations much older than us, they are more or less equal to us in the universal shared mother knowledge. As we begin to seek other life, as do they. Her age is determined in astrological ages, if we observe the stars, then by delivery of her stars, we will learn from our mother, and from the divided cells she creates we may find our siblings. Her love is all, her purity corrupted only as a sacrifice to love.

Reference Materials

- The Cult of The Black Virgin - Ean Begg
- Cybele, Attis, and the Mysteries of the Suffering Gods - Evgueni A. Tortchinov
- The Twelve Signs of the Zodiac – T Subba Rao
- The Unknown God – Fred J Mayers
- History of England – Dr Goldsmith
- The Nag Hammadi Gnostic texts